iContractor1

2nd Edition

iContractor1

2nd edition

Constructing Your Perfect Life by Remodeling YOU from the Inside Out!

jon m ketcham

When people think of Iowa, they often think of cornfields and miles upon miles of flatlands. However, Davenport, Iowa, where I went to Chiropractic school, is actually quite hilly in places, particularly where it rises to the west of the mighty Mississippi River. Main Street is paved with brick and is particularly steep between Sixth and Eighth Streets. One day, while walking to my classes, I came upon a crowd of fellow students who had all gathered to watch an old Excalibur car struggling to make the grade. Now, if you've never seen one of these, they look remarkably similar to the car from the movie "Chitty, Chitty, Bang, Bang." (1) So, of course, I joined them in watching. Struggle though it may, the car was not advancing. Several of the gathered students were eager to assist the driver with their advice. Their varied suggestions only seemed to further confuse him.

The first suggestion was to apply salt to the roadway. Even though it was the middle of July, the thought was that the memory of the long winter had to be addressed and dealt with. Salt was liberally spread out, but to no avail.

The second suggestion was to step harder on the gas pedal. Everyone remembered the story of "The Little Engine That Could" and, perhaps the driver just wasn't trying hard enough. (2) Stepping harder on the gas pedal produced lots of noise and smoke. Everyone cheered at the increased effort, but still no progress was made up the hill.

Another student suggested backing all the way down the hill, purging any unnecessary weight and trying again with a running start. But, once this was done, the car could not even climb as high as it originally had.

One professional looking student suggested that the driver was in the wrong type of car for such a climb and suggested the driver grow up and change vehicles.

Religious counsel was offered by a passing minister, who stated that his Book said it was sinful to want to climb the hill in the first place. The driver was instructed that he should donate his vehicle to a more worthy cause.

Fortunately, before the driver had a chance to change vehicles or give up the climb altogether, one rather simple-minded student spoke in a calm but deliberate tone. She stated: "Clear the salt from the roadway and leave it be. Ease up on the gas. Keep the car you have and continue your climb. But, first, take off the emergency brake!" The driver did as instructed and made the climb without further incident. (3) Far too many people never reach their goals; they never accomplish their dreams, because they go through life with their emergency brake on.

<u>iContractor1</u> will teach you a simple 3-step process that will lay the foundation to making all of *your* dreams come true. You truly can have, be and do anything you want if you will follow the blueprints inside. Now, get to work!

iContractor1

iContractor1: Constructing Your Perfect Life by Remodeling YOU from the Inside-Out! **by jon m ketcham**

© 2012, 2nd Edition 2020 by **Jon M. Ketcham**. All rights reserved.

No part of this publication may be reproduced or transmitted in any form or by any means, mechanical or electronic, including photocopying and recording, or by any information storage and retrieval system, without permission in writing from author or publisher. The exception would be in the case of brief quotations embodied in the critical articles or reviews and pages where permission is specifically granted by the publisher or author.

Disclaimer: The Publisher and the Author make no representations or warranties with respect to the accuracy or completeness of the contents of this work and specifically disclaim all warranties, including without limitation warranties of fitness for a particular purpose. The fact that an organization or website is referred to in this work as a citation and/or a potential source of further information does not mean that the Publisher or the Author endorses the information the organization or website may provide or recommendations it may make. Further, readers should be aware that internet websites listed in this work may have changed or disappeared between when this work was written and when it is read. Please see following page for additional disclaimer.

ABIYD Publishing Company
www.ABIYD.com

Cover Illustrations by Jon D. Ketcham

ISBN: 978-0-9905511-6-4
Library of Congress Control Number: 201293538

10 9 8 7 6 5 4 3 2 1

Motivational & Inspirational / Metaphysics / Mysticism

Second Edition Printed in Saegertown, PA. United States

Additional Disclaimer

The information and strategies provided by **iContractor1** are intended to educate, inform, empower, amuse and inspire you on your personal journey towards excellence: goal-setting/goal-achieving, growing your business/bank account, achieving optimal health/wellness, improving your relationships and maximizing your quality of life. It is clearly not intended to replace a one-on-one relationship with a licensed health care professional and it is definitely not offered up as a substitute for proper medical or chiropractic advice, diagnosis or treatment. Proper diagnosis and advice relative to treatment of any existing health conditions cannot be made through a book and is well beyond the scope of any information offered. The intent of the author is solely to offer information of a general nature to assist you on your quest for spiritual and emotional well-being. The author will not accept any liability, perceived or otherwise, for the improper application of any principles taught through this text. In the event you, the reader, choose to use or apply any of the strategies in this book for yourself, which is your constitutional right, the author and the publisher assume no responsibility for your actions.

iContractor1

Dedication

To my wife Lisa, so beautiful in every way! You are my "ideal" soul mate and my best friend; my most challenging student and my most demanding teacher; the one who saw my potential and continued to believe in me when all others had long since given up. Forever One!

iContractor1

Preface

My story is truly an underdog story, one that includes overcoming much heartache and seemingly insurmountable odds.

- Born into a struggling middle class family, the last of 4 boys
- Lost mother to cancer at age 16
- Watched father go bankrupt, losing the family business and the family homestead
- Personally went broke 3x in 4 years
- Recovered from near death illness at age 36
- Ruptured appendix, peritonitis & septicemia; the same ailment that claimed the life of Houdini!
- Nearly became homeless at age 38
- Transformed life from one of abject squalor and hardship into one of prosperity and abundance

I have been on borrowed time since 2001. But, the truth of the matter is that we are all on borrowed time. Some of us are just more aware of it than others.

My story includes a decade-long intensive study of nearly 100 books, several dozen audio programs and a dozen or so videos while turning my life around. Journeying through the depths of hell, experiencing colossal loss, despair, illness and lack, I found myself! Having gone through way more and holding on way longer than most could or would, I have learned so much. And, what I have learned can and will help millions more to believe in their dreams and, by default, to believe in themselves!

iContractor 1 is not an autobiography. Rather, it is a "how-to" handbook that takes the Law of Attraction from a "whoo-hoo", feel-good kind of wishing to a real-life, nitty-gritty application program that can shave decades off of the learning curve for living the life of your dreams.

Do yourself a favor. Read the book. Buy the tee-shirt. Buckle up & enjoy the ride! Install this APP into your daily life and finally realize your true potential. Remember, Always Believe In Your Dreams!!!

Introduction

What I am about to share with you is *not* new information. It has been available, in various forms, throughout the ages. Furthermore, anyone could figure out everything that I will tell you I have discovered for themselves. If we all could be quiet long enough to hear the wee small voice inside each and every one of us, the voice of God if you will, this information would be common knowledge to us all. Unfortunately, very few ever hear it; and even fewer heed it. And, while the principles I will share with you are quite simple in nature, putting them to use on a consistent basis is very difficult, even seemingly impossible for most to do.

To the novice, it may appear as though applying the Law of Attraction to summon your dreams and desires is easy to do. Let's face it, the teachers in the movie, The Secret, certainly made it appear easy! (1)

Similarly, anyone watching Michael Jordan make free throws or George Winston playing piano could also mistakenly conclude that making free throws and playing piano are easy. What they would be overlooking, however, are the thousands (yes, thousands) of hours of diligent, consistent practice that went into getting to that skill level in the first place. How many hours? According to Malcolm Gladwell, author of Outliers, The Story Of Success, "researchers have settled on what they believe is the magic number for true expertise: *ten thousand hours*." (2) Furthermore, the time spent under the watchful eye of a skilled and knowledgeable coach or teacher could be missed.

Notice that I qualified that last statement: a "skilled" and "knowledgeable" coach or teacher. When I went bankrupt for the first time, I was put in touch with a consultant who told me all of the wrong things to do. After reviewing a videotape of the healthcare classes I was teaching to new patients, this particular consultant supplied me with a whole laundry list of "urgent" recommendations: my monogrammed maroon clinic tops were too passionate of a color and needed to be replaced with soft colored polo shirts immediately; my hair, which I wore in a well-kept ponytail was way too long and needed to be cut much more conservatively; my closely manicured beard was unprofessional and needed to be shaved off at once and my speaking abilities were poor and ineffective so the healthcare classes needed to be discontinued. Finally, the icing on the cake, I was so devoid of personality that I was told I should apologize pre-emptively to any new patients for my complete and total lack of any social skills, telling them that I am this way because I take their healthcare so seriously. Apparently, I dressed like shit, I looked like shit, I spoke like shit and, when it came right down to it, I was shit!!! I followed every single one of these recommendations and went broke two more times over the next three years. Why? Because all of these "recommendations" focused on changing the external environment rather than focusing on the real problem, my internal environment! A truly skilled and knowledgeable coach or teacher would have focused their attention there. You see, moving from "serial failure" to prosperity is ALL about up-leveling your internal state of being.

Yes, applying the Law of Attraction to achieve all of your dreams is relatively simple to do. But, at least initially, it is NOT easy. Like any learned skill, it requires much more effort and practice early on; all the better under the watchful eye of a skilled and knowledgeable coach or teacher. Only once mastered does it appear easy.

It's *easy* to take things so *simple* for granted. But, that doesn't mean that things so *simple* are *easy*! Often, it is quite the opposite.

iContractor1

Table of Contents

Disclaimer — *viii, ix*

Dedication — *xi*

Preface — *xiii*

Introduction — *xv*

Table of Contents — *xix*

Chapter 1 "It's All Your Fault!" – The Reason For The Season — 1

Chapter 2 Mirrors, Windows, Doors & Light — 5

Chapter 3 The Law Of Attraction — 15

Chapter 4 Thoughts — 23

Chapter 5 Feelings — 31

Chapter 6 Actions — 39

Chapter 7 Supporting Worthy Goals   49

Chapter 8 Always Believe In Your Dreams Coaching (SM) Method   55

Chapter 9 Afflatus   65

Afterward   71

About the Author   73

Connecting with the Author   75

Other Books by jon m ketcham   77

Appendix A: Recommended Reading List   79

Appendix B: Recommended Audio / Video Programs   85

Appendix C: Email Daily quotes and newsletters   87

Appendix D: Constructive Concepts: Words to live by from iContractor 1   89

Appendix E: Always Believe In Your Dreams
Coaching (SM) Method Charts   *97*

A Quick Note Concerning Quotes   *109*

Sources   *111*

Bibliography   *119*

Notes   *123*

iContractor1

Chapter 1

"It's All Your Fault!" – The Reason For The Season

Paramount to living the life of your dreams is recognizing and acknowledging the role you have played in your current set of circumstances. Are you a creature of circumstance or a creator of circumstances? Are you a victim or a victor? Do you blame others or do you claim your results? "Groanership" or ownership?

Why does this matter? If you see yourself as a creature of circumstance, a victim who blames others and always groans to others about their stream of bad luck, you might just as well run down to Wal-Mart and buy yourself a Magic 8-Ball. Or, you could just sit around and do nothing as your life continues to happen to you! But, if you are ready to take charge and live the life of your dreams, then it's time to recognize and acknowledge your role in the results you currently see before you.

Everything you have in your life currently is there because you attracted it there, either by active choice or by default, by failing to make a choice. Everything you experience as the world around you, your external world, is nothing more than the mirrored *reflection* of who you have been on the inside, your inner world, through your thoughts, feelings / emotions and actions. There is no "luck", only the results you have created for yourself, either by intent or by default. You have to CLAIM your ownership of your results in life and not BLAME others for them.

You may be thinking, "Sure Doc, that's easy for you to say. You've got it easy! You're a doctor. You don't know how hard I struggle and how hard I have it." And, you are right. I don't know you or your struggles. But, let me tell you a little bit about mine and perhaps we can find some common ground.

I went bankrupt three times in four years. During the first episode, my wife miscarried our third child. During the second episode, my appendix ruptured, I developed peritonitis and went septic. I nearly died and still have residual health issues related to it to this day. Homelessness became a very real and likely possibility during the third episode. But, don't get me wrong. I am not sharing this with you in some distorted attempt to garner your pity. No, I share this with you because I created all of it! It was all my fault! It wasn't the product of bad luck. Neither was it contagious, as many of my relatives and former friends thought! Today, after a decade-long, trial-by-fire, intensive study of the principles of success, I have a thriving practice, multiple income streams and am truly living the life of my dreams. I created all of that as well. Both were created by the thoughts I entertained, the feelings / emotions I expressed and the actions I took (or failed to take).

> *One of my good friends always says, "Things don't just happen; things happen just."*
> **Jim Rohn (1)**

If you are not willing to at least entertain the possibility that you contributed to your current state of affairs, you can't expect things to change for you. You will just keep re-experiencing the same kinds of situations and events over and over and over again. Real, lasting, meaningful change cannot take place until you adequately ponder and start to answer the following question: How did I create, or at least contribute to, my current situation? You don't need to be able to fully answer it right away. But, you must be open to the possibilities.

If you are not willing to discard the victim card, you can't ever expect to play a winning hand! Drop the victim card and play the hand you are dealt!

> *Start from wherever you are and with whatever you've got.*
> **Jim Rohn (2)**

While some, perhaps most, will take offense to this chapter, it can be colossally life changing for you. If it truly is "all your fault", if you truly are "the reason for the season", then that means you can also change things to be however you desire! It was this very realization that led me on my quest and ultimately enabled me to turn my life around. Now, it's your turn!

Chapter 2

Mirrors, Windows, Doors & Light

Your outer world is simply a reflection of your inner world.
T. Harv Eker (1)

Legend has it that Socrates could often be found sitting outside the gates of Athens where he could greet strangers. One day, a man came up to him and said, "I am thinking about moving to Athens. What are the people who live in Athens like?" Socrates replied, "I'd be glad to tell you. But, first tell me about the people where you are from." To this, the man went into a tirade, "Oh, they are just horrible. Nobody cares about anyone but themselves. No one will help another who is in need, yet they are always minding others business. They will rob you blind, if you let them. I am leaving only cold-hearted enemies behind." Socrates, in his infinite wisdom replied, "Well, you might as well continue your search elsewhere because you will find it the same way here." So, the sour man continued elsewhere on his journey.

Some time later, another traveler casually approached Socrates and asked, "I am considering moving to Athens. Can you tell me a little about the people who live there?" Socrates again replied, "I'd be glad to. But first, tell me about the people where you are from." This time, the second traveler smiled warmly and said, "The people of my village are wonderful! Everybody looks out for their neighbor because, after all, we are all connected aren't we? We are all like family there. I am only traveling so I can expand my horizons and meet the neighbors and family members that I have yet to introduce myself to." Socrates smiled back and said, "Welcome to Athens brother. You will find the people here to be just like you have described."

> *You don't get in life what you want.*
> *You get what you are.*
> **Les Brown (2)**

Why did Socrates embrace the second traveler while rejecting the first? Was it not possible that the two travelers came from very different types of cities? Or, did Socrates understand something far deeper than that? Perhaps he knew that other people could only reflect back to you your own beliefs about yourself and your environment. People merely mirror back to you who you were on the inside, based upon your prior thoughts and feelings or emotions. They can only reflect back to you what you have already put out there. Most likely Socrates knew that, in both situations, the traveler would find the city of Athens to be just like the places they came from. He knew that, wherever you go, there you are: thinking the same kinds of thoughts, feeling the same kinds of feelings or emotions and taking the same kinds of actions, thus causing the same kinds of situations to be reflected back unto yourself. Denying the first man entrance to the city of Athens was like preventing weeds from overtaking his garden.

> *Your dominant thoughts create your conditions.*
> **Napoleon Hill (3)**

So, where do our thoughts and feelings come from? Contrary to popular belief, our thoughts and feelings do not exist solely as random, spontaneous reactions to our surroundings; at least they do not have to! In fact, we can actively choose to think and feel, or not think and feel, in certain ways. We can choose our response to any given circumstance. Viktor Frankl, a survivor of four WWII concentration camps of the Holocaust, wrote in <u>Man's Search For Meaning</u>, "Everything can be taken from a man but one thing: the last of the human freedoms – to choose one's attitude in any given set of circumstances, to choose one's own way." (4) In other words, no matter what happens to you, you can *always* choose your response, your thoughts and feelings. It is like the ancient Greek philosopher Epictetus stated, "Men are disturbed not by things, but by the views they take of them." (5)

Socrates asked the two travelers about their respective cities because he knew that our attitudes, our perceptions, our worldview are like windows through which we view our world. The condition of our windows colors our view and simultaneously announces it for all the world to know. Ralph Waldo Trine wrote in his masterpiece <u>In Tune With The Infinite</u>, back in 1897, "cease your complaining…keep your pessimism, your 'poor, unfortunate me' to yourself, lest you betray the fact that your windows are badly in need of something. But know that your friend, who keeps his windows clean, …lives in a much different world from yours." (6) Our attitudes, perceptions and worldview serve as the windows through which we announce our current level of being to the world. Other people serve as mirrors, reflecting that state of being back to us.

> ***In my Father's house***
> ***are many rooms.***
> **Bible (7)**

Ask any four year old what they want to do on any given day and their world is chock full of possibilities. Unfortunately, as we get older, our lives get busier and more scarred by disappointment, illness and loss. As such, we tend to see fewer and fewer opportunities around us. It can seem as though there are no open doors of opportunity left for us to enter.

The reality, however, is that opportunity is always around us, and it always has been. There are no fewer possibilities available to the adult than to the child. We just have to get back in touch with our inner child to see them. In fact, Joseph Campbell states, "When you follow your bliss, doors will open where you would not have thought there were going to be doors, and where there wouldn't be a door for anybody else." (8)

Even in the face of failure, there are always opportunities. Neale Donald Walsch, author of the <u>Conversations With God</u> series states, "All endings start something better. It is inevitable. When one door closes, another does open." (9) Just like Napoleon Hill stated back in 1937 in his classic <u>Think And Grow Rich</u>, "Every adversity, every failure and every heartache carries with it the seed of an equivalent or a greater benefit." (10) Problem is, we tend to get so wrapped up in our losses that we forget to look for the benefit(s) contained therein. That does not eliminate their existence however.

All of these doors of opportunity represent who you might become. But, unless you look for them and step through them, nothing changes. Everybody experiences loss and fear, but not everybody allows themselves to become paralyzed by it. Learning to Feel The Fear And Do It Anyway ®, as Susan Jeffers titled her wonderful book, can mean the difference between staying stuck versus growth and enjoyment. (11)

> ***When one door closes, another opens, but we often look so long and so regretfully upon the closed door that we fail to see the one that has opened for us.***
> **Alexander Graham Bell (12)**

Where we get mixed up is in thinking that these opportunities are, somehow, separate from us; on the other side of these doors, so to speak. Contrary to the opinions of the masses, the collective consciousness, we are not physical beings yearning for a spiritual connection. Rather, we are spiritual beings having a physical experience; an experience that often deceives us. Genesis 1:27 states, "God created man in His own image." (13) John 8:12 states, "I am the light of the world. He who follows Me shall not walk in darkness, but have the light of life." (14) John 10:30 continues, "I and My Father are one." (15) Separation from God is often described as "being in the dark." Survivors of near-death experiences all talk about going towards or returning to the light. When people figure out the solution to a long perplexing problem, they often say they have "seen the light." The truth is, we are all beings of light; light resonating with a dense vibrational form.

Putting it all together, we see that our attitudes and perceptions are the windows that color the light that emanates from within us. Others simply mirror back to us that which we have already emanated. And, the real clincher? Opportunity is not on the other side of the doors; it is within you already in the form of your innermost dreams. That is why we say that your dreams are INspired. Doors of opportunity do not open to reveal to you what is outside of you. Doors of opportunity open to let your light shine out! Your dreams are your gifts from God. Following those dreams is your gift to God.

> *Launch yourself on every wave,*
> *find eternity in each moment.*
> **Henry David Thoreau (16)**

Denying your innermost longings is like closing your doors and putting a self-imposed prison upon your soul. Dr. John Demartini says, "The greatest cause of illness, disease and death is not living your dreams." (17) It will eat you from within.

We all use mirrors to check our appearance before going out in public, to make sure we look ok. We can use our metaphorical mirrors, other people and how they treat us, to check how we are doing in life. Do others generally treat us with respect, compassion and love? Or, does their behavior towards us suggest that we are not being all we can be? Perhaps the windows of our soul are in need of a good cleaning, streaked with the sludge of "aintitawfulism," pessimism, worry and fear. And what of our doors of opportunity? Are we able to recognize them in all of their bounteous splendor? Are we courageous enough to step through them when we do recognize them? Or, do we let self-doubt and prior loss paralyze us from taking action?

- **Mirrors – other people and how they treat us**
- **Windows – our thoughts (attitudes, perceptions & worldview)**
- **Doors – our innermost dreams**
- **Light – our true nature**

Motivational speaker and success guru Les Brown tells a wonderful story about a man who goes for a walk and passes by a house where people are gathered together around a porch. Along with them, the man sees and hears a dog whining and moaning in apparent pain. Curious, and rather concerned, the man approaches the gathering of people and asks, "What is wrong with that dog?" "That dog is laying on a nail that has protruded through the floorboard of the porch," he is told. "Then, why doesn't he get up and move to a different spot?" the man asks. "Because it doesn't hurt enough to make him move. It only hurts enough to make him complain," is their reply. (18) That protruding nail is your buried hopes and dreams, your many doorways of opportunity waiting to be opened. How bad does it have to get before you are spurred into action, not just complaint?!?

Far too many people die with their light still locked up inside them. They ignore their true needs and innermost longings because they fear what others will think of them; they fear the possibility of trying and failing; they feel unworthy and unable to afford what they truly desire. Leading lives of quiet desperation, their inner light dims until there is next to nothing! Every time you stifle your inner passions and deny yourself your dreams, a part of you dies. The time to pursue your dreams is NOW! When would NOW be a good time to start? If you are not growing, you are dying. Why not choose to stop dying? Stop denying your inner most longings. Listen to your heart. Fan that light back into a glorious flame. Follow your dreams and finally start to really live! Always Believe In Your Dreams!!!

iContractor1

Chapter 3

The Law Of Attraction

> *All individuals have become what they are because of their dominating thoughts and desires.*
> **Napoleon Hill (1)**

According to the law of attraction, like attracts like: like thoughts, like feelings, like actions. Like attitudes of mind are naturally and powerfully drawn together. Birds of a feather really do flock together. We attract whatever we desire or expect based upon the dominant thoughts, feelings and actions that permeate our existence. We can do this intentionally, literally creating our dream life by selectively choosing our thoughts, feelings and actions. Or, we can allow whatever random thoughts and feelings occur in reaction to our surroundings to form a hodge-podge of noise that seemingly victimizes us by default.

Our thoughts, feelings and actions are forces that broadcast into the ethers *who* we are being on the inside. Furthermore, this broadcasted message goes out and finds like frequencies or vibrations which get drawn back to us one hundred fold; kind of like a massive, magnified *reflection* from the mirror of

God. These frequencies or vibrations show up as the external situations and events of our lives. When we react spontaneously to the external situations and events, we typically broadcast even more like frequencies and attract even more like situations and events to ourselves. However, if we respond intentionally, by selectively thinking specific thoughts, feeling specific emotions and taking specific actions, we can unlock the power to change the external situations and events that we draw to ourselves.

> *Life isn't happening to you;*
> *life is <u>responding</u> to you.*
> **Rhonda Byrne (2)**

By holding ourselves, whatever present conditions may be, continually in a specific thought and emotion, we set into motion forces that eventually bring us into synch with that specific condition. This can be a positive thing or a negative thing, depending on the nature and orientation of our dominant thoughts and emotions. Changing our internal level of being ultimately changes what gets *reflected* back to us, not just through the responses of others, but through the situations and events themselves. In order to change any or all that you see around you, externally, you must first change what you are putting out there from internally!

The Law of Attraction is not new. In fact, there are various texts and writings, going back hundreds of thousands of years that convey a solid awareness and understanding of this law. The underlying premise of the Law of Attraction is that we create our own circumstances in life, either by active choice or by default. Not making a choice is still making a choice, by default. Einstein said, "There are only two ways to live your life. One is as though nothing is a miracle. The other is as though everything is a miracle." (3) Similarly, there are really only two schools of thought concerning life as it pertains to your results: your health, wealth, relationships and so on. One is as though everything that happens to you is at the whim of luck or chance. The other is as though you, and you alone, are completely responsible for your results. One school of thought paralyzes, the other empowers. Recognizing ourselves as creators of circumstance (manifestors) rather than creatures of circumstance (victims) means taking 100% ownership of our responsibility for our lot in life. While somewhat scary and sobering, this is also tremendously empowering. Anything that you have done (or attracted) that is not to your liking can be undone. And anything that you have yearned for without success can now be yours. But first, you must come to terms with your role in the external situations and events of your life. Everyone and everything in your life is there because *you* attracted them there. *You* placed the order with *your* thoughts.

You paid the freight with *your* feelings and emotions. *You* signed for the package with *your* actions. *You* and only *you*! If you want a different result on the outside, you must first become a different you on the inside.

> ***All of us are self-made, but***
> ***only the successful will admit it.***
> **Earl Nightingale (4)**

> ***All that we are is a result***
> ***of what we have thought.***
> **Buddha (5)**

Crucial to maximizing your use of the Law of Attraction to manifest your dreams is making sure that your thoughts, feelings and actions are all operating in perfect alignment and synchronicity. Within certain parameters, what you think about you bring about! Now, obviously, there must be some conditions on this principle. Otherwise, every adolescent boy would have the entire cheerleading squad wanting to date them and every teenage girl would have entire fashion stores in their closets. Come to think of it, that sounds pretty much like my daughter's closet now, but back on topic. So, what parameters empower your thoughts? Your thoughts are either empowered or decimated by your feelings; your emotions and belief system. An adolescent boy may think about and dream about dating the entire cheerleading squad. But, deep down, he is unlikely to *feel* it a real possibility for himself. In fact, he may be too scared to even talk to any girls! His feelings contradict, and thus negate, his thoughts relative to the Law of Attraction. In order to truly attract our desires and manifest our dreams, we must *think* about what we want **and** we must *feel* that it is possible for us, *feel* that we deserve it and *feel* that it is likely to take place (belief).

Finally, our actions must occur in synch with and in support of our most dominant thoughts and feelings. The arena of action is often greatly misunderstood. Some critics have gone so far as to say that it is an area that is neglected entirely by Law of Attraction teachers. This is not really the case though. The "actions" to be taken in pursuit of one's dreams have more to do with "how" something is done than with the actual specific "whats" that are to be done. Back in 1910, Wallace Wattles wrote in The Science Of Getting Rich, "People do not become wealthy (successful) by doing certain things. People become wealthy (successful) by doing things in a certain way." (6) In other words, it's the "hows" not the "whats" that matter most! And, as T. Harv Eker states in Secrets Of The Millionaire Mind, "*How* you do anything is *how* you do everything." (Emphasis added) (7) Change the "hows" to change your results!" For instance, the actions to be taken in pursuit of one's dreams have to include acting "as if" you already had your heart's desire. The reason for this is two-fold. It demonstrates or affirms your belief **and** it creates the feeling of having your desire now. Again, it all boils down to creating and maintaining a certain **feeling** consistent with achieving your dreams.

In regards to thoughts, feelings and actions, your feelings reign supreme. They always, always, always win. Let me explain. Most people have all three of these components in perfect synch. They think negative thoughts, they have negative feelings and they take little or no action. Their lives suck and they'll tell you all about it in great, agonizing detail. They make no effort to change and attempt to drag anyone else down with them that might aspire to loftier ideals. They are dream vampires and will suck the life out of any dreams you may have if you let them!

Then, there are those who struggle. They may try to improve the quality of their thoughts, engaging in positive thinking. They set goals and even study personal development, often becoming "self-help" junkies. However, then they manage to self-sabotage every single time. Where many go astray here is they focus on the three letters in the middle of the word 'believe': L I E. They want to believe things will go well and in their favor; but, deep down, they feel it's a lie. They don't feel things will go well and in their favor. Doubt wins out! Their negative feelings counter their positive thoughts. They want their lives to change, badly so! But, on a visceral (gut-feeling) level, they don't feel it is really possible or likely for them. They may feel undeserving. So, they stay stuck!

You can't just think harder to "beat" negative feelings such as fear, worry and lack. Anything you resist persists. The harder you try to beat them, the stronger and more persistent they become. Your focus on them intensifies them. It's like when you get a song stuck in your head; sometimes a song that you don't even like. The more you try not to hear that song, the louder it seems to play in your head. The only way to make it go away is to replace it with a different song, maybe one you do like. Rather than beating these negative thoughts, you have to replace them. Positive emotions and negative emotions cannot co-exist; one replaces the other. Therein lies the beauty. By choosing to focus your energy on one, it automatically replaces the other. Positive emotions, like gratitude for what you already have, create a different energy. Start by making a list of all of the things you already have in your life that you are grateful for. This list, if you dig deeply enough, should be quite lengthy. Then, once you get practiced at it, a quick daily review of small segments of your list should be all that is necessary to generate the feeling tone of gratitude within your being. Even if you haven't got all the things you want, then at least be grateful for the things you don't have that you don't want!

This brings us back to the "hows" not the "whats". What actions you take do not matter nearly as much as how you take them. Coming from a place of gratitude and positive expectation, regardless of what specifically you are doing, will bring your dreams to life much quicker. Coming from a place of lack and unworthiness will choke the life right out of your dreams, however. Strive to create and maintain feelings consistent with achieving your dreams in any and all actions you engage in.

Boiling it all down to its inner, core essence, using the Law of Attraction to accomplish your dreams could be summed up in one six-word statement: **"Thoughts, feelings, actions supporting worthy goals."** Your thoughts, your feelings and your actions all in alignment with, in support of, your goals. And, for true success, your goals must be goals worthy of accomplishing. Thus, **"Thoughts, feelings, actions supporting worthy goals!"**

Chapter 4

Thoughts

Thoughts become things!
Mike Dooley (1)

Where do our thoughts come from? As stated earlier, our thoughts do not exist solely as random, spontaneous reactions to our surroundings; at least they do not have to. We can choose to think anything we want to. Critical to this process is learning to tune out those things we do not want to attract, those things that do not serve us, while tuning in to those that do.

With multiple news channels running 24/7, it is easy to become inundated with stories of gloom and doom. And, while it is one thing to stay informed, it is quite another to wallow and drown in the glut of negative news stories. Bear in mind too that there are some of us who choose not to watch the news at all! Once those negative images get flashed before your eyes, even if only for a brief second, they can become quite difficult to erase from the video screen of your mind. At least with a newspaper, you have the option of skipping over a story once you have seen the headline. Learn to be very selective with what information you allow to enter into your mind. This applies to all forms of media: video, audio, pictures and text. Often times, when we learn of a negative event, we are tempted to think to ourselves, "Can you imagine that?" Don't do it! Don't let that toxic story become a part of you.

In my town, every year, they hold a "homelessness night" where people can come and experience first hand what it's like to be homeless for one night. While I can certainly sympathize with the plight of the homeless, this event is far more likely to create more homelessness than it prevents. Having nearly been homeless myself, after the third time I went broke, I can tell you that teaching people how to think, feel and act homeless is *not* the solution. Far better would it be to bring in someone who had gotten themselves off of the streets to share what their thought process was that enabled them to overcome homelessness. Teach people how not to become homeless in the first place!

> *Rags, tatters and dirt are always in the mind before being on the body.*
> **Ralph Waldo Trine (2)**

In the Conversations With God book series, written by Neale Donald Walsch, he documents the "inspired" answers he received while dialoguing with God. (3) Similarly, in the movie The Answer Man, the lead character is an author who wrote a popular book where he "made up" the answers to his questions to God. (4) In both cases, real and fiction, multitudes of people flock to them, thinking that they have a direct line to God. Many turn to their religious leaders thinking the same thing. In all instances, they are correct! These people do have a direct line to God. However, so do each and every one of YOU! Furthermore, these other people cannot give you the answers to your questions, not completely. Only you can get the complete answers to your questions by going direct to God yourself! Anyone can do this by turning inward, accessing and listening to the *wee small voice within*. As B.J. Palmer, the developer of Chiropractic termed it, "the Bigness of the Fellow Within." (5) All of us have this connection. It is the Source of all inspiration and intuition. People like Neale Donald Walsch don't need a bunch of followers who worship them. What they do need, and want, are students who will learn from them and do for themselves.

> *Let your heart guide you.*
> *It whispers, so listen closely.*
> **Littlefoot's mother's last words (6)**

Henry David Thoreau, author of <u>Walden – Life In The Woods</u>, retreated to the woods to escape the "noise" of everyday life so he could better commune with that wee small voice within. (7) This is thousands of times more relevant today than when he wrote it. We are surrounded by a constant barrage of external "noise" from our cell phones, iPods, internet, TVs, and so on. Society today is so "connected" to this hodge-podge of noise that we get literally no reprieve from it during any of our waking hours. It is interesting to note that many of the amenities and luxuries of today likely came from others tapping into this wee small voice of inspiration. Unfortunately, these same amenities and luxuries tend to drown out and block our ability to tap into and hear our own wee small voice, our connection to God.

Blocking outside distractions in order to access the wee small voice within is not unique to Thoreau. Men such as B.J. Palmer, Thomas Edison and Albert Einstein all spent considerable time sitting quietly thinking. B.J. Palmer received many of his ideas for innovation from what he called "thought flashes" that came to him during these thinking sessions.

The magic is inside you.
There ain't no crystal ball.
Dolly Parton (8)

Start spending time thinking. Think about what you want, not what you don't want. Remember, what you focus on expands. Focus on what you want. Choose your thoughts carefully. Put your filters up to keep the toxic thoughts out.

If you are having trouble accessing the wee small voice within, start by selectively choosing your thoughts. Pick several short, positivity statements, called positive affirmations, that you want to make true for your reality. These affirmations can be repeated over and over to yourself anytime you feel the need to drown out any negative thoughts that are streaming through your mind.

One way to become more aware of the thoughts you are thinking is to start paying close attention to the "story" that you tell to others about yourself. For example, "I can't afford that", "I'm no good at _____(fill in the blank)", "I always mess things up", "I'm too _____(fill I the blank) for that", etc.

> *Argue for your limitations,*
> *and sure enough, they're yours.*
> **Richard Bach (9)**

Maybe it's time to write a *new* story about yourself; one that actually supports your grandest dreams and aspirations. Change your story, change your thoughts, change your life!

Look at your life as though it is a play which you are currently writing/scripting through your thoughts, feelings, emotions, expectations and actions. You write the script. You hold the casting calls. You attract all of the players.

Everyone and everything that you encounter in your life is there because you attracted/scripted it. Everyone and everything plays their role 100% perfectly according to the script you have written. If you don't like a particular act, re-write/re-script it! You don't get to choose who will fill which roles. You merely write the script and the perfect actors show up in the perfect scenery. Anyone/anything that plays or played a role you dislike is still performing 100% perfectly according to the script you previously wrote. If you don't like the role they play or played, change your script (i.e. your thoughts, feelings, expectations, etc.). Further, you don't have to invite any particular actors back for a repeat or an encore performance. Change the script. Again, you cannot control who will fill which roles. All you can do is re-write the script to include new or different roles.

Anything man can imagine,
man can make real.
Jules Verne (10)

Your subconscious mind cannot tell the difference between current events and future, imagined events. This is where the magic of visualization springs from. However, it also cannot tell the difference between current events and past events. Every time you re-live a past hurt, a past-perceived failure, you resuscitate it and give it life anew. If you want to create real, lasting change in your life, stop re-animating (re-living) past hurts and start re-scripting (visualizing) new successes.

One way you might apply this exercise and make it more meaningful is to write an annual newsletter about your life and all you have accomplished in a year. But, remember; write it as though it has already happened, one year in advance!

Most people are an aggregate of worry, lack, doubt and negativity directed haphazardly in a multitude of directions. However, by actively deciding to do so, we can focus our thoughts and energies in one consistent direction. William James says, "the greatest discovery of my generation is that human beings can alter their lives by altering their attitudes of mind." (11) What do you think?!?

Thoughts – Summary

- Learn to be very selective with what you allow to enter your mind.
- Block out the toxic overload
- Quiet your mind and listen for the wee small voice within.
- Change your "story".
- Script a new you.
- Write an annual newsletter one year in advance.

Chapter 5

Feelings

Whenever your feeling is in conflict with your wish, feeling will be the victor.
Neville Goddard (1)

As we stated earlier in regards to thoughts, feelings and actions, your feelings reign supreme. They always, always, always win! Charles Haanel wrote in The Master Key System, way back in 1912, "the law of attraction … is another name for love…there is no getting away from the Law of Love…feeling is desire and desire is love." (2) By reducing this down to a simple, mathematical proof where:

- A = Law of Attraction
- B = love
- C – feeling
- D = desire

A = B (Law of Attraction = love), D = C (desire = feeling) and D = B (desire = love)

If A=B and D=B, then A=D (Law of Attraction = desire)

And…

If A=D and C=D, then A=C (Law of Attraction = feeling)

The Law of Attraction = <u>feeling</u>

Thus, you can sum up the Law of Attraction in one word: **FEELING!**

Thoughts may well become things, as what you think about comes about, but *only* if you fuel it with feeling; deep, gut-level feeling.

Emile Coué was a French Pharmacist and Psychologist in the late 1800s who was a strong advocate for autosuggestion or affirmation. The Coué formula called for regular repetition of the phrase, "Every day, in every way, I get better and better!" (3) While this affirmation can be very powerful indeed, Napoleon Hill was quick to point out in <u>Think And Grow Rich</u>, "the mere reading of words is of no consequence --unless you mix emotion, or feeling, with your words." (4)

The idea behind affirmations is to replace an old belief with a new belief, saying them over and over and over again until you believe them. However, whether you repeat them five times or five bazillion times, if you don't eventually believe them, or <u>feel</u> them to be true, they will *not* help! Instead, the very lie that they become creates a powerful, negative feeling that blocks you from your dreams.

> *I said, and said, and said those words.*
> *I said them. But I lied them.*
> **Dr. Seuss (5)**

The keystone to putting the Law of Attraction to work for you in the pursuit of your dreams revolves around replacing and/or up-leveling your underlying feelings about what you are thinking, saying and doing. Many have heard the saying, "fake it 'til you make it," as a way to describe acting "as if." Les Brown says, "Sometimes, you have to believe in somebody's belief in you until your belief kicks in." (6) But, do not kid yourself. The goal here is changing your belief system at a visceral, gut-level.

Replacing or up-leveling your feelings is not as complicated as it might at first appear. You can not just beat feelings of fear, worry, doubt, lack and so on, especially when these feelings are engrained so deeply from your childhood, your upbringing, your religion, your prior experiences and so on. Remember, what you resist persists. Your focus on them, attempting to silence or stifle them, only makes them grow stronger. However, you can replace these negative feelings with a different, positive set of feelings. Positive feelings and negative feelings cannot co-exist. By actively choosing to feel one way, you actually cancel out the other. You can choose your feelings as surely as you can choose what you are going to wear every morning. There are numerous positive feelings you can choose from such as happiness, love, gratitude, etc. However, gratitude is probably the simplest one for most people to implement. Start by making a list of 101 things already in your life that you are grateful for. As you compile this list, note how it feels to truly be in a state of gratitude. Then, any time you want to go through your affirmations, make sure you get yourself into this feeling tone first, by reviewing your list or compiling it anew. Eventually, you can practice feeling gratitude in advance for that which you seek. Initially, however, just be sure that you can genuinely create the feeling of gratitude for the NOW! Otherwise, your fears and doubts will disconnect any positive thoughts and actions from their true power.

> *Poverty consists in feeling poor.*
> **Ralph Waldo Emerson (7)**

Remember, your thoughts, feelings and actions all play a role. But, your feelings set the overall tone. Think of your feelings as the train track that sets your course. Your thoughts and actions serve as the fuel cells for the train engine. Positive or negative feelings determine where the track is headed. Your thoughts and actions serve as the fuel cells made either of coal (if they are in alignment with your feelings) or of water (if they are in opposition to your feelings). The one can power the train engine, really ramping up its power and speed. The other douses the fire and slows the engine to a crawl, sometimes even stopping it cold. But, only the direction of the tracks (your feelings) determines your ultimate destination.

Another way to replace or up-level your feelings is through a process called neural linking. This method is a favorite of John Assaraf, one of the teachers of <u>The Secret.</u> (8) What you do is this. Think back to a specific time period or event where you were particularly successful and on top of your game. Everybody has some of these. In fact, it would be a good idea for you to take the time to compile a written "accomplishments resume" of all of your accomplishments that you can think of. You can categorize it, if you want to, by different time periods. For instance: High School, College, and Graduate School. Or, by decades: teens, 20s, 30s, etc. Any way that you compile it is ok. The point is to make the list in the first place. Then, select the most memorable event from your list.

John Assaraf talks about one particular basketball game where he felt totally "in the flow," guarding a much larger player and successfully limiting his ability to score, all the while scoring himself, seemingly, at will. He describes it as one of the most emotional moments of his life and one that he can drop into the "moment" of and relive in a heartbeat. He can, at a moments notice, close his eyes and still see the sights, hear the sounds and feel the thrill of that game. Pick an event of your own, one that still elicits strong, positive memories and feelings for you. Then, just as you get yourself into the depths of re-living (and re-feeling) the bliss of that moment, recite, either out loud or in your head, your affirmation(s); in particular, the one(s) that are toughest for you to believe. Pairing a strong, positive emotional, visceral event with your affirmation(s) like this supercharges your belief system by creating the feeling tone you need to make your affirmations feel true to you.

Another, similar method, would be to compile a list of joyous, blissful times or events in your life. For example, your first kiss, attending the school of your dreams, courting your spouse, the birth of your children, etc. Just like in the above example, once you get yourself into the depths of re-living (and re-feeling) the bliss of that moment, recite your affirmations.

Feelings - Summary

- The Law of Attraction can be summed up in one word: FEELING.
- Create a Gratitude Journal of 101 things that you are grateful for NOW.
- Create an Accomplishments Resume of all of your prior successes.
- Create a Happiness Resume of joyous, blissful times for you
- Sample Affirmations:
    - Every day, in every way, I get better and better.
- Practice neural linking.

iContractor1

Chapter 6

Actions

Wallace Wattles wrote in The Science of Getting Rich that people do not become wealthy by doing certain things. Rather, people become wealthy by doing things in a "certain way." (1) We stated earlier that what actions you take do not matter nearly as much as how you take them. Bear in mind, how you do anything is how you do everything! Thus, it is the "hows" not the "whats" that ultimately determine your results.

What does this all mean? What are those "certain ways"? What are those all-important "hows"?

Numerous texts such as In Tune With The Infinite, by Ralph Waldo Trine (1897), The Science of Getting Rich, by Wallace Wattles (1910), Think And Grow Rich, by Napoleon Hill (1937) and The Secret, by Rhonda Byrne (2006) all use the term "action" to refer to changing and controlling your feelings. (2)(3)(4)(5) Most people think *externally* when taking action, attempting to change their environment (spouse, partner, job, geography, etc.). However, the action that is called for here is mostly *internal*, changing your thoughts, feelings and the way you carry yourself. Whatever situation you find yourself in, first seek to be specific about choosing the feelings you allow yourself to entertain. Choosing and controlling your attitudes of mind or feelings is the first and most powerful action step you can take toward realizing your dreams.

In other words, whatever you are already doing, learn to be specific in choosing the attitudes of mind or feelings you express. Let's say, for example, that you are unhappy with your current employment. Rather than quitting your job (a "certain thing"; a "what") in the hope of finding something better, first you must work on the attitudes of mind or feelings (a "certain way"; a "how") that you are bringing to your current line of work. If, hypothetically speaking, you had your dream job right now, what would your attitude of mind be? How would you feel? How would you carry yourself? How would you speak? How would you interact with others? How would you dress? How would you act? Learning to "conduct" yourself now (remember the train analogy?) *how* you would if you already had your dream fulfilled is the key. Changing jobs while still "conducting" yourself as you always have (changing the "certain things" or "whats" but NOT changing the "certain ways" or "hows") guarantees that you will remain stuck attracting the same old situations and events.

> ***Unless you change how you are, you will always have what you've got.***
> **Jim Rohn (6)**

My wife's grandparents spent their entire lives in search of an apartment that was to their liking. They would find a place that was "just perfect" only to become quickly disillusioned and unhappy with it. Thus, the search would begin anew for a better place. Every two to three years they would move and this pattern repeated itself their entire lives, *seventy years together*. All told, they lived together in nearly *thirty* different places!

What is the *one* constant amidst all of the variables of *your* life? Regardless of where you live, where you work, where you vacation and so on, the only constant is *you*! Wherever you go, there *you* are: thinking the same thoughts, feeling the same feelings and emotions, taking the same actions and attracting the same results. It's always you and the results of your consistent choices.

How many times have you known someone, maybe even you yourself, who, after repeatedly encountering the same struggles over and over and over again, felt the need for a "change of venue"? And so, they, or you, moved to a new locale, a new job, a new relationship and so on only to ultimately find themselves in the same situation, with the same kind of struggles yet again? Why?!? Again, wherever you go, there *you* are. **In order for things to change and improve, you don't need a "change of venue." What you need is a "change within you!"**

One powerful way to change the way you perceive any given situation is to make a habit of always looking for the benefits that that situation provides you. There is no such thing as a negative without a positive, a challenge without a gift. As stated previously, Napoleon Hill says in Think And Grow Rich, "Every adversity, every failure, every heartache carries with it the seed of an equivalent or a greater benefit." (7) Going back to the example of current employment that you find unpleasant, what *do* you like about it?!? Focus on the benefits, making a list of as many things as you can come up with. How does your current employment serve you and move you closer to your dreams? Aim for at least fifty benefits you receive from your current employment. They are there; you just have to look for them. Work to generate the feeling tone of gratitude for your current employment by creating and focusing on this list. Start raising your expectations. Know that this current employment will lead to something better down the road. Dr. John Demartini says, "Until you clearly define what you love and have a strategy to pursue it, it is wise to love what you do." (8) This is a tremendous opportunity to become clear, perhaps for the first time, about what you *do* actually want! Act "as if" what you are currently doing, whatever that is, actually matters. It does! Act "as if" what you are currently doing is taking you closer to your dreams. It is taking you somewhere either way! Act "as if" what you are currently doing is a necessary step in taking you toward your dreams. It is!

A colleague once told a wonderful story about a particular time when he was crossing the border into another country. Nearly all of the tollbooth operators were very stiff and somber, all lined up in their little booths. However, the tollbooth operator at the booth he was going through was strikingly different. He was animated, jovial and seemed to be in the midst of a powerful dance performance that emanated from his very soul. When my colleague asked him what made him so different from all of his co-workers, this man stated that he was a dancer and that working the tollbooth was enabling him to continue to work his way to Broadway. All of his co-workers, on the other hand, hated their jobs and were just putting in the hours for a paycheck. He commented further how it was as if they were already dead, all lined up in their coffins. This particular tollbooth operator, however, was already a dancer, from the very core of his being.

Do what you love and
love what you do.
Dr. John Demartini (9)

Similarly, Mark Victor Hansen, co-author of the <u>Chicken Soup For The Soul</u> mega-series of books, tells of how he handled bankruptcy early in his career. Unable to find work other than day labor unloading toilet tissue off the back of a railroad car, he showed up wearing a white trench-coat and patent leather shoes. When questioned by his co-workers, why he came dressed like that for menial labor, he replied, "I ain't staying long!"(10)

Learn to think, feel and act *how* you would if you had already realized all of your grandest dreams! Learn to BE the person who has already succeeded, before it manifests in the seen. Nearly everyone in America today is familiar with the name Arnold Schwarzenegger: former bodybuilding champion, blockbuster movie star and former Governor of California. However, few realize the obstacles he overcame in pursuit of his dreams. None of it happened by chance. When Arnold first came to America, his goals seemed rather absurd. While he was hugely successful in bodybuilding, his prospects for movie stardom and politics seemed a bit far reached. His first movie, "Hercules In New York", was a poorly written B-movie, at best. And, because Hollywood execs felt no one would ever be able to pronounce, let alone spell, his last name, his name was changed to Arnold Stang for the pic. Furthermore, they felt no one would ever understand his thick accent; so another voice was dubbed in replacement of his. Not the best confidence builders, for sure. Yet, when interviewed around that same time by sportswriter Steve Chandler, Arnold calmly stated that he was going to be the number one box-office star in all of Hollywood! Arnold went on to say, "It's the same process I used in bodybuilding. What you do is create a vision of who you want to be, and then live into that picture, as if it were already true." (11)

Similarly, another important action step to adopt when following your dreams is the practice of "right speech." I first heard of this concept through the writings of Frank Zane, three-time Mr. Olympia winner. He talked about the need for care in choosing the words you let yourself speak. While preparing for one of his competitions, he found himself regularly uttering the phrase "that pisses me off!" Not only did it sound crass, he ultimately suffered a freak accident while sunning himself poolside where he slipped and cut his urethra, jeopardizing his life and decimating his hopes for that particular contest. (12) I too learned this lesson the hard way. Under major financial stress, on my way to going broke for the second time, I uttered the phrase, with much passion and emotion, "I feel like I am going to explode!" Sure enough, approximately two months later, I nearly died from a burst appendix! Get in the habit of only uttering that which supports your grandest dreams. If your dreams were already realized, if you had everything your heart desires, how would you speak? Speak that way now!

Another means of acting "as if" involves making room in your life for that which you seek to attract. For instance, let's say you are looking to attract your soul mate. If you currently sleep in the middle of your bed, where is your soul mate supposed to sleep? Where does your soul mate keep their stuff? **Make room in your life for your soul mate by making room for your soul mate in your life.** Start sleeping on one side of your bed. Make room in your closet for your soul mate's clothes. Clear space in your dresser, or make room for another dresser, for your soul mate's belongings. This point is important enough that it bears repeating. **Make room in your life for your dreams by making room for your dreams in your life.** Nature abhors a vacuum. Therefore, create a vacuum and watch it get filled!

Bottom line, start thinking, feeling and acting the way you would if you had already fulfilled your dreams. Go back and re-read this chapter and the chapter on "Feelings" until you understand them fully. When you understand how to perform your actions in the "certain way" necessary for success; when you finally know "how" to be to get "what" you want, the keys to the kingdom will be yours. Then as it says in Luke 11:9-10, "Ask, and it will be given to you; seek and you will find; knock, and it will be opened to you." (13)

iContractor1

Actions – Summary

- Do what you love and love what you do. (14)
- Make a habit of always looking for the "benefit(s)" of any given situation.
- Act "as if."
- Practice "right speech."
- Make room in your life for your dreams by making room for your dreams in your life.

Chapter 7

Supporting Worthy Goals

Success is the progressive realization of a worthy ideal.
Earl Nightingale (1)

As we discussed earlier, your thoughts, feelings and actions all play a role in how your life turns out. Feelings play the most influential role and can negate the effects of your thoughts and actions when they are in conflict. Having all three components aligned in harmony, supporting your goals, provides the most bang for your buck. When it comes to your goals, we stated that they should be "worthy" goals. What exactly does this mean, to be following "worthy" goals?

Tran•scen•den•tal – adj.

(1) going beyond ordinary limits; surpassing
(2) being beyond ordinary or common experience, thought or belief (2)

On April 16th, 2011 athletes from as far away as Alabama, New York and Ohio, as well as numerous local athletes, converged on Saegertown Jr./Sr. High

School's auditorium stage to compete in the inaugural run of "The Reach for The Ring", a drug-tested N.M.A. Bodybuilding, Figure and Bikini Championship. Many months of arduous preparation went into getting each and every one of the athletes, who ranged in age from early twenties to late sixties, ready for the stage. And, while only a select few earned top honors and the elusive Pro card, every one of the athletes overcame tremendous obstacles and odds just to be there.

Randall J. Strossen, editor-in-chief of <u>Milo: A Journal For Serious Strength Athletes</u>, coined a wonderful term: "Transcendental Levitation." (3) Basically, he says that when evaluating the results of any structured weight-training regimen, whether for bodybuilding, fitness, powerlifting, Olympic lifting, strongman, Highland Games, other sports or even just general recreation, the real value comes as a result of the process itself. Goal-setting / goal-getting, striving and overcoming obstacles changes you; so much so that who you become in the process far exceeds the original goal or intent. Hence, the transformative power of the struggles against gravity up-levels you not just physically, but mentally and spiritually as well: "Transcendental Levitation!"

> *If you know what to do to reach your goal, it's not a BIG enough goal.*
> **Bob Proctor (4)**

A similar phenomenon often follows serious illness or failure (e.g. bankruptcy). Both illness and failure have a way of forcibly stripping away all of our false personas and defense mechanisms; laying bare for all the world to see, our weaknesses, frailties and shortcomings. These events, and how we choose to respond to them, provide an opportunity for us to re-connect with our inner, higher selves. Pondering the questions: "Who am I? Why am I here? What do I stand for?" begins the process of re-claiming your true self; "Transcendental Reclamation", if you will. Honoring your innermost needs and desires up-levels your level of being and provides inspiration and example for others. Consider people like Gandhi, Mother Teresa, Martin Luther King and His Holiness the Dalai Lama.

Every one of us matters. It's up to each one of us, individually, to decide why. Mother Teresa states, "Each of us feels that we are just a drop in the ocean, but the ocean would be less without that missing drop." (5)

It is not necessary to lift weights or become ill or fail at something to improve oneself or transcend one's current level of being. (Although, I do have experience with all three!) Jim Rohn, America's Leading Business Authority, says that one of the greatest lessons he ever learned was when his mentor told him to "set a goal of becoming a millionaire for what it will make of you to achieve it. Set a goal that will make you reach for the stars." (6) He goes on to say, "the greatest value in life is not what you *obtain*, the greatest value in life is what you *become* along the way." (7) Part of what makes goal-setting / goal-getting, striving and overcoming obstacles so powerful and so transformative is the leap of faith that it requires us to make. None of us knows for sure, upon embarking on any new journey, what the outcome will be. As such, it requires us to believe in ourselves, often well in advance of any concrete evidence in favor of such. In doing so, we catch glimmers of our own unlimited potential. Furthermore, the "distraction" of goal-setting / goal-getting, striving and overcoming obstacles gets us out of our own way. This process connects people, sometimes for the first time ever, with the *feeling* of their own intrinsic worth.

> ***Be who you are and say what you feel,***
> ***because those who mind don't matter***
> ***and those who matter don't mind.***
> **Dr. Seuss (8)**

So many people spend their whole lives trying to fit in, to be like everybody else, and not make waves. But, as I often say, **conformity is the death knell to success.** We come in all shapes, sizes, colors and orientations and that is part of the beauty of being human. Trying to fit everyone into the same mold robs us of our own unique contribution to society.

> *Do not try to be anything but what you are, and try to be that perfectly.*
> **Francis de Sales (9)**

Any time we base our self-worth or value as a human being on our appearances, or worse, someone else's opinion of our appearance, we are in trouble. You have value just because you are! The real value in goal-setting/goal-getting, striving and overcoming obstacles comes as a direct result of the process itself. By persevering against the odds, you get a glimpse of your true worth and inner power as a human being: "Transcendental Realization". As Neale Donald Walsch, author of the Conversations With God book series states, "I have learned to trust the process of life, and not so much the outcome. Destinations have not nearly as much value as journeys." (10)

> *Most people fail in life not because they aim too high and miss. Most people fail in life because they aim too low and hit. … And, many don't aim at all! Many just survive.*
> **Les Brown (11)**

iContractor1

Chapter 8

Always Believe In Your Dreams Coaching (SM) Method

At Always Believe In Your Dreams, we teach and inspire our clients to believe in their dreams; and, by default, to believe in themselves. Tantamount to their success is following the Always Believe In Your Dreams Coaching methodology (SM) which revolves around a simple 3-step process:

- **Step one:** Decide your "whats"
- **Step two:** Up-level your "hows"
- **Step three:** Act "as if"

Decide "What" [the tangibles]

> *How do you live if you don't know what you want on your sandwich? How do you get married, have kids, buy a house if you don't know what you want on your sandwich?!?*
> **John Pinette (1)**

Step one: Decide your "whats"

Decide exactly what your dreams are! Put them in writing, stated in the affirmative only. (What you want, not what you don't want.) Be as specific and detailed as you possibly can. You are trying to paint a graphic picture, with words, that will create an indelible image for your subconscious to easily visualize.

Most people are really good at creating graphic visualizations that they focus and dwell upon regularly. Unfortunately, they are usually all negatively oriented. Let me demonstrate:

In my chiropractic practice, I always start off patient encounters with a question such as, "Good morning Mrs. Smith. How are you doing today?" Or, "Good afternoon John. How are you feeling today?" When they are doing well, or better than they had been, patients will usually respond with something similar to "not too bad, I guess." Or, "I'm getting by." But, when they are not doing well, patients often paint the most vivid, colorful pictures of their dismay. "Oh, Doctor," they will say, "I feel like I'm getting zapped by 220 volts of electric current surging through my lower back." Or, "Doctor, it feels as though I have been impaled by a red hot fire poker every time I take a step. It just kills me!" Now, which responses are ambiguous and without feeling? And, which responses draw you in and make you part of the experience? Some patients paint such exquisite pictures of their pain and suffering, yet barely give a classified ad presentation to their improvement. Similarly, so many people create vivid, detailed masterpieces of their lack and perceived failures but barely give a footnote mention to their successes. Sages throughout the ages have taught us that "what you focus on expands" and "energy flows where attention goes." Now, which do you think will move you closer to realizing your dreams: focusing on (and thus magnifying) your lack and perceived failures or focusing on (and thus magnifying) your successes?

The first step toward realizing your dreams is to first have a dream to realize! What do you want? What does success look like to you? Most people are afraid to clearly define what they want in life. They are afraid it is going to cost them something. Or, they are afraid of what others will think of them if they follow their dreams. Or, they are afraid of trying and failing, so they don't bother trying at all! In fact, if you asked anybody off the street, "Do you know what you want in life? What do you really want?" it is unlikely that 2% of the population could answer and describe it fully.

And make sure to state only what you do want, not what you don't want. It is OK to start there, if you must, but quickly re-state your wants in the positive or affirmative only. Your subconscious does not hear the "don't", only the "want." Focusing on what you "don't" want can have disastrous consequences. Several years ago, my family and I went to a new, family-owned burger joint for dinner.

Wanting to try one of their "famous" burgers, but somewhat overwhelmed by the myriad of available condiments, I told our waitress that I wanted everything but "I don't want pickles and mustard." When our order came, you guessed it; my burger had only pickles and mustard on it! State what you *do* want, **not** what you don't want!

So, again, the first step in realizing your dreams is to clearly define your dreams. Be specific. Be exquisitely specific. Write it down! For example, if a person says, "I want more money" and they find a penny, dream answered, right? How much money? If a person says, "I want to lose weight" and they drop one pound, dream again answered, right? How much weight? By when? What do you look like after this specific weight loss? How do you feel after this specific weight loss? What benefits / advantages does it give you? How will you even recognize your success when it presents itself if you never bothered to define it in the first place?

Rather than focusing on your past (glory days) or perhaps your present set of circumstances (how bad it may be), spend time creating, painting vivid pictures with your mind of how you would like your ideal life to look. Devote time to this daily; really put your heart into it. Peter Daniels, one of the richest men in Australia, performs a similar exercise and credits it with turning his life around. In fact, Mr. Daniels devotes an entire day a week just to thinking and visualizing his tomorrows. Interestingly, he has the dubious distinction of having gone broke three times within five years before turning his life around. (2) For the record, I went broke three times within four years, but I always was an overachiever! Einstein used a similar strategy, actually doing his pondering in a special thinking chair. Even Steve, from Blue's Clues, utilizes a designated "thinking chair." (3)

Most people spend more time planning out their vacations than they do planning how they want their lives to look! If you want to rise above ordinary, you have to be willing to do what the ordinary don't!

> *Everything you think, say and do needs to become intentional.*
> **Jack Canfield (4)**

Let's say, for example, that you are hoping to attract your soul mate. What does your soul mate look like? Are they short? Tall? Heavy? Light? Curvy? Athletic? Are they educated? To what level? Do they have a particular career? What are their priorities? What is their value system? What is their worldview? What kind of personality do they possess? What kinds of interests do they have? What is their temperament? Do they have kids? Do they want kids? What are their religious views? Philosophical views?

You cannot be too specific here. What are you looking for exactly? Do not be afraid to state exactly what you want. How else will you be able to recognize them, or *not* them, when you encounter such? Decide "what" then "put the vapor on the paper." Write it down! This, by the way, is the easy part.

Up-level "How" [the intangibles]

Step two: Up-level your "How's"

What exactly is a soul mate anyways? Strictly speaking, a soul mate is the one(s) who resonates perfectly with your soul; the mate to *your* soul. However, everyone you are attracted to and connect with resonates (or resonated) with who you are (or were) at that time. Not only that, but I would go so far as to say that they resonate (or resonated) 100% perfectly with who you are (or were) at any given moment in time. We are always attracting our ideal mates. It's just that the one(s) who are an ideal match for us at any given time are not always to our liking. Therefore, if you want to find/attract your "ideal" soul mate, you must first become the match to that which you seek. If you are not satisfied with whom you have been attracting, then you need to up-level your own soul development first! As Deepak Chopra states, "However good or bad you feel about your relationship, the person you are with at this moment in time is the 'right' person, because he or she is the mirror of who you are inside." (5)

Now for the $60 million question: Is who you are currently *being* consistent with who you are hoping to attract? Remember, like attracts like. The only way to attract a better relationship is to bring a better *you* to the table! **In order to attract your true love, your "ideal" soul mate, you must first become that which you seek.** This is the hard part; prohibitively so for most. What is the level of *your* conviction?

Act "as if"

Step three: Act "as if"

As mentioned previously, this has more to do with how you carry yourself, your attitude of mind, than any particular action steps. It's about *being*, not *doing*. It's about *how* you live your life, not just *what* you do. It's about those nebulous "certain ways" which are infinitely more important than any "certain things."

If you already had your "ideal" soul mate in your life, how would your life look and feel? How would you feel first thing in the morning, every morning, knowing that you had your "ideal" soul mate beside you? What kinds of thoughts would fill your mind? How would you dress? How would you talk? What would you talk about? Would your walk have more of a spring to it: an easy gait that conveys jubilation, gratitude and love? Start thinking those kinds of thoughts, feeling those kinds of feelings and taking those kinds of actions now!

Make sure that the "story" you are telling others about yourself actually supports your dream of finding and attracting your "ideal" soul mate. Become aware of your speech habits and strive to utilize "right speech." Forgive yourself for past errors. When you know better, you do better. Change your "story" and script a new you!

Make room in your life for your "ideal" soul mate by making room for your "ideal" soul mate in your life. Previously, we suggested sleeping on one side of your bed, keeping your clothes to one side of your closet and making room for another dresser. This is only the beginning. Let your creative juices flow here. There are an infinite number of fun ways to "make room" for your "ideal" soul mate. And remember too, it is not just about making "physical" room. Make TIME for the activities you plan to do with your "ideal" soul mate. Speaking of activities, what kinds of activities would you be pursuing or participating in if you already had your "ideal" soul mate in your life? Take your life off hold and start pursuing those activities now! This is the most fun part!

Consistency and congruency are the keys. Consider them "the C & C of success!" For example, seeking your "ideal" soul mate while simultaneously engaging in one-night stands is not congruent. The very act of going out, trolling for whomever you can find, sends a very different message than wanting to find your "ideal" soul mate. Hopefully, you wouldn't engage in these behaviors if you were in a loving, committed relationship with your "ideal" soul mate. Acting how you would act if you already had your "ideal" soul mate in your life is the key.

Those already partnered with someone, but not satisfied with their relationship can instantly up-level it by working on themselves, improving *who* they be on the inside. It's like the employee who never goes the extra mile, doing the absolute minimum requirement, bad attitude and all, yet wanting to go into a newly opened management position who says, "If I became a manager, *then* I would do more and go the extra mile." No they would not! Going back to T. Harv Eker's quote, "*How* you do anything is *how* you do everything." (6) Make sure that the anything and everything you do are consistent and congruent with your desires NOW.

3 – Step Process - Summary

Summarizing the Always Believe In Your Dreams Coaching Methodology (SM):

(1) Decide "WHAT" - [tangibles]

　　WHAT does your ideal dream life look like?

(2) Up-level "HOW" - [intangibles]

　　HOW does your ideal dream life feel? (attitudes of mind)

(3) Act "as if"

　　Create the *feeling* of HOW to manifest the WHAT

Chapter 9

Afflatus

Af•fla•tus – n.

(1) inspiration; an impelling mental force acting from within
(2) divine communication of knowledge (1)

Many are familiar with the Parable of the Talents, which appears not once, but twice in the New Testament. (2) According to Scripture, a prosperous man divides his wealth amongst three individuals, "each according to his own ability", while he leaves on a long journey. Upon his return, he gathers the three individuals together to see what they have done with the gifts he entrusted to them during his absence. Two of the individuals have taken what they were given and used it to create even more. This pleases the prosperous man and both individuals are richly rewarded. However, the third individual fears the prosperous man. He accuses the prosperous man of having wealth that was not earned or deserved. As such, he returns to the prosperous man only what he was given, no more, having kept the gift hidden and buried during the prosperous man's absence. Angered by the third individual's unfounded accusations and non-use of the gift, the prosperous man takes it from him and gives it to one of the individuals who have shown that they will make proper use of it. "For unto everyone that hath shall be given, and he shall have abundance; but from him that hath not shall be taken away even that which he hath."

Matthew 25:31-46 continues on with the admonition, "for I was hungry and you gave me food to eat, thirsty and you gave me drink, a stranger and you took me in, naked and you clothed me, sick and you visited me...as surely as you have done it unto one of the least of my brethren, you have done it unto Me." (3)

In the Parable, the "talents" or "minas" are traditionally interpreted to be a unit of money for exchange. Money, however, is nothing more than a form of energy. The "talents" or "minas" could just as easily be interpreted to mean any gifts from God that we are intended to make use of and multiply for the good of humanity; "the least of my brethren." These are the wide range of abilities, skills and service capabilities we are each uniquely gifted with. These are the innermost dreams and aspirations we all have within our soul.

An unfulfilled vocation drains the color from a man's entire existence.
Honore de Balzac (4)

All of us have dreams, aspirations and longings. These are our gifts from God that we are meant to multiply and share with humanity. They first express themselves as some of our main interests, hobbies and passions. When we are kids, we overflow with dreams. These dreams are expressions of our unique relationship with God. As we get older, our dreams tend to get suppressed by a multitude of factors like peer pressure and not wanting to stand out as "different." Parents, teachers and society all seem to just want us to fit into a uniform, predictable, controllable, "un-offensive" mold. This multifaceted drive for conformity, focusing us on our weaknesses, leaving no child behind, buries our "talents" and creates a homogenized, fruitless society. Your dreams are not just for you! They are meant to be expressed and increased for the good of us all. Rollo May, the distinguished psychiatrist, says in Man's Search For Himself, "The opposite of courage in our society is not cowardice, it is conformity." (5) And, as I have said before, conformity is the death knell to success.

Be yourself; everyone
else is already taken.
Oscar Wilde (6)

Following your dreams is not a selfish endeavor. It is the most selfless act you will ever commit! When you follow your dreams the whole world benefits. Oliver Wendell Holmes says, "The greatest tragedy in America is not the destruction of our natural resources, though that tragedy is great. The truly great tragedy is the destruction of our human resources by our failure to fully utilize our abilities, which means that most men and women go to their graves with their music still in them. " (7)

Find your afflatus! Quiet your mind and listen for the wee small voice within. In the words of Howard Thurman, theologian, educator and civil rights leader, "Don't ask what the world needs. Ask what makes you come alive, and go do it. Because what the world needs are people who have come alive." (8)

Use this book as your blueprint to a new you! Everything you need to know to follow your dreams is contained herein. If, after reading and re-reading this tome three times, you still feel you need additional help, hire a skilled and knowledgeable life coach to guide you on your journey. Sometimes, as Les Brown says, "You need some coaching…you can't see the picture when you are in the frame." (9)

> *It is never too late to be*
> *what you might have been.*
> **George Eliot (10)**

Remember always: You Matter! Your dreams matter! And you are worthy *and* capable of following and achieving *all* of your dreams right NOW!

> ***Your life is an occasion. Rise to it!***
> **Mr. Magorium (11)**

iContractor1

Afterward

Everything in this book may be wrong.
Richard Bach (1)

Everything contained within this book has been learned through years of focused study and multiple episodes of arduous, near-crippling struggle. "Been there, bled that!" sums up my life experiences the best. While I cannot guarantee you that all I learned will prove true for you, it certainly has been so for me. Go ahead and try the methods contained herein. I challenge you to prove me right!!!

iContractor1

About the Author

For more than a decade, jon has immersed himself in the study of success, high achievement and wealth. Culling the salient points from authors spanning several thousand years, he has boiled the Law of Attraction down to its core essence and formulated his simple, three-step process for achieving all of your dreams, which he then implemented as his

Always Believe In Your Dreams Coaching (SM) Methodology.

jon lives in "wooded bliss" on 35 acres of dense forestland in Meadville, Pennsylvania. He has two beautiful, gifted children: a seventeen-year-old son who is a talented science fiction author and a fourteen-year-old daughter who aspires to be an attorney. He shares his home with 2 basset hounds, one chihuahua, seven cats, two guinea pigs and a cockatiel!

Update 2020:

Eight years later, both of jon's children are all grown up. His 2 basset hounds and his chihuahua are long gone. He, and his beautiful wife Lisa, share their home now with eight cats, one guinea pig, one bunny, six chickens and a dove.

Connecting with the Author

Websites:
www.AlwaysBelieveInYourDreams.com

Social Media:

    Instagram:
        @hearton4lifting
        @jon.m.ketcham

    Facebook:
        Jon M. Ketcham

    LinkedIn:
        jon m ketcham

    YouTube Channel:
        Jon Ketcham

    Twitter:
        @jon_m_ketcham

    Pinterest:
        jon m ketcham

iContractor1

Other Books by jon m ketcham

The Reach for the Ring - *my 42 year love affair with the iron*

Ask Me Who I Was - *audacious brain farts on life, death and immortality*

The Golden Role - *Just Be Nice!*

The "Zero's Journey" - *A Modern-day Survival Guide to Weathering Accidental Enlightenment*

iContractor1

Appendix A

Recommended Reading List

The book you don't read won't help.
Jim Rohn (1)

Jim Rohn, known as "America's Foremost Business Philosopher", (recently deceased) used to lament how when a highly successful speaker would recommend to an audience of hundreds of thousands of people a particular book that really turned their life around, so few would actually go out and buy the book (let alone read it). He called it one of the great mysteries of life. How true! It's never how much a book costs you. Rather, it's how much it'll cost you if you don't read it!

In that spirit, I have put together a recommended reading list of some of my favorite (and most useful to me on my journey) texts. This list is by no means comprehensive of all of the wonderful works that have influenced my thinking.

The Law Of Attraction:

(1) In Tune With The Infinite by Ralph Waldo Trine (1897)
(2) The Science Of Getting Rich by Wallace Wattles (1910)

(3) The Master Key System by Charles Haanel (1912)
(4) Think And Grow Rich by Napoleon Hill (1937)
(5) The Secret by Rhonda Byrne (2006)
(6) iContractor 1 by Dr. Jon M. Ketcham (2012)

All six of these books relate the EXACT same message using the verbiage of the time when written. All six are excellent sources for deepening your understanding of the Law of Attraction.

Further Law Of Attraction "themed" books:

(1) The Law Of Attraction by Esther and Jerry Hicks
(2) Conversations With God (Books 1,2 and 3) by Neale Donald Walsch
(3) The Answer by John Assaraf & Murray Smith
(4) Infinite Possibilities by Mike Dooley
(5) The Attractor Factor by Joe Vitale
(6) In Search Of The Invisible Forces by George Addair
(7) Tao Te Ching by Lao Tzu

Success Manuals:

(1) The Power Of Focus by Jack Canfield, Mark Victor Hansen, Les Hewitt
(2) The Success Principles by Jack Canfield

(3) Leading An Inspired Life by Jim Rohn
(4) How To Reach Your Life Goals by Peter J. Daniels
(5) Twelve Pillars by Jim Rohn and Chris Widener
(6) Dare To Win by Mark Victor Hansen

Motivational:

(1) Jonathan Livingston Seagull by Richard Bach
(2) Illusions: The Adventures of a Reluctant Messiah by Richard Bach
(3) Oh, The Places You'll Go! by Dr. Seuss
(4) Chicken Soup For The Soul Series by Jack Canfield and Mark Victor Hansen
    a. Any title, especially the first book
    b. Chicken Soup For The Soul Living Your Dreams
    c. Chicken Soup For The Unsinkable Soul
(5) Happy For No Reason by Marci Shimoff
(6) Happier Than God by Neale Donald Walsch
(7) Feel the Fear and Do It Anyway ® by Susan Jeffers

Attitude / Mindset / Perceptions:

(1) Man's Search For Meaning by Viktor Frankl
(2) Acres Of Diamonds by Russell H. Conwell
(3) The Power Of Perception by Marcus Bach
(4) The Structure Of Scientific Revolutions by Thomas Kuhn

(5) The Holographic Universe by Michael Talbot
(6) Maze Of Life by Barry Bittman, M.D. and Anthony DeFail, M.P,H

Money Consciousness:

(1) The Richest Man In Babylon by George S. Clason
(2) Secrets Of The Millionaire Mind by T. Harv Eker
(3) Rich Dad, Poor Dad by Robert T. Kiyosaki with Sharon L. Lecter
(4) How To Make One Hell Of A Profit And Still Get To Heaven by Dr. John F. Demartini
(5) The One Minute Millionaire by Mark Victor Hansen & Robert G. Allen
(6) The Trick To Money Is Having Some! by Stuart Wilde

Self-Esteem:

(1) Miss Phillips, You Were Wrong by Peter J. Daniels
(2) The Aladdin Factor by Jack Canfield and Mark Victor Hansen

Quote Books:

(1) The Treasury Of Quotes by Jim Rohn
(2) Messiah's Handbook by Richard Bach

(3) Notes From The Universe by Mike Dooley
(4) Mark Victor Hansen's Treasury Of Quotes by Mark Victor Hansen
(5) Excerpts From The Treasury Of Quotes by Jim Rohn
(6) Excerpts From The Treasury Of Quotes by Brian Tracy
(7) Zig Ziglar's Little Book Of Big Quotes
(8) Success Quotes For Achievers by Success Magazine
(9) Treasury Of Quotes by Chris Widener
(10) Todd Dodge Lessons From Sports
(11) Excerpts From The Seeds Of Greatness Treasury by Denis Waitley
(12) Identity Passport To Freedom by Stedman Graham
(13) As A Man Thinketh by B.J. Palmer

Note that books # 4 through 12 are pocket-sized gift books.

Misc.:

(1) The Chiropractic Story by Marcus Bach
(2) The Bigness Of The Fellow Within by B.J. Palmer
(3) Lost Horizon by James Hilton

iContractor1

Last, but not least:

As recommended by Jim Rohn:

(1) How To Read A Book by Mortimer J. Adler & Charles Van Doren

Appendix B

Recommended Audio / Video Programs

Audio:

(1) The Challenge To Succeed by Jim Rohn (4 cds)
(2) Unlimited Riches by Mark Victor Hansen (8 cassettes)
(3) How To Become A Millionaire by John Earl Shoaff (1 cd)
(4) The SGR Program by Bob Proctor (17 cds)
(5) The Strangest Secret by Earl Nightingale (1 cd)
(6) Life Visioning by Rev. Michael Bernard Beckwith (6 cds)
(7) Masters Of The Secret by Bill Harris (8 tracks)
(8) How To Think Bigger than you ever thought you could think by Mark Victor Hansen (6 cassettes)
(9) The Art Of Exceptional Living by Jim Rohn (6 cds)
(10) Teachers Of The Secret (5 cds)
(11) Live Full & Die Empty by Les Brown (1 cd)
(12) Step Into Your Greatness by Les Brown (1 cd)
(13) The Secret Soundtrack (1 cd) and Audiobook (4 cds) by Rhonda Byrne

iContractor1

(14) Dreams Don't Have Deadlines by Mark Victor Hansen (6 cds)
(15) Million Dollar Mindset by James Arthur Ray (6 cds)
(16) The Science Of Success by James Arthur Ray (6 cds)
(17) Holosync audio program from Centerpointe Research Institute
(18) The Science Of Getting Rich (audiobook)
(19) The Power (audiobook) by Rhonda Byrne

Video:

(1) The Secret
(2) Being In Heaven by Michael Domeyko Rowland
(3) Teachers Of The Secret
(4) Live Full And Die Empty by Les Brown
(5) Step Into Your Greatness by Les Brown
(6) The Moses Code by James F. Twyman
(7) The Bucket List
(8) The Answer Man
(9) Conversations With God
(10) The Adventures Of Sharkboy And Lavagirl

Appendix C

Email Daily Quotes and newsletters

Like vitamins for your mindset, these websites deliver daily, weekly, bi-weekly and / or monthly inspirational quotes and newsletters that you can sign up to receive to help you stay positive and focused on living the life of your dreams. Most people start their day with a daily dose of mindset poison by watching the news or reading the negative-themed stories in the newspaper. Be different from the rest to bring out your best!

Daily:

- www.BobProctor.com (sign-up for Free Daily Inspirational Message)
- www.BrianTracy.com (sign up for Quote Of The Day)
- www.NealeDonaldWalsch.com – click on [Daily Inspirational Email signup]
- www.Simpleology.com (sign-up for Simpleology Daily)

Weekly:

- www.YourSuccessStore.com
    - Your Achievement Newsletter

iContractor1

- o Jim Rohn Weekly Newsletter
- o Seeds Of Success (excerpt from Success Magazine)
- o Denis Waitley Newsletter
- o Ron White Newsletter
- www.theSecret.tv/ - signup for The Secret Scrolls

Biweekly:

- www.HappyForNoReason.com - Marci Shimoff Newsletter
- www.JackCanfield.com - Success Strategies Newsletter

Monthly:

- www.SusanJeffers.com - Monthly Newsletter

You can also follow us on Facebook and Twitter where we post inspirational quotes.

Appendix D

Constructive Concepts: Words to live by from iContractor 1

1) Do yourself a favor. Read the book. Buy the t-shirt. Skip the ride!
2) The truth of the matter is that we are all on borrowed time. Some of us are just more aware of it than others.
3) Moving from "serial failure" to prosperity is ALL about up-leveling your internal state of being.
4) It's *easy* to take things so *simple* for granted. But, that doesn't mean that things so *simple* are *easy*! Often, it is quite the opposite.
5) You have to CLAIM your ownership of your results in life and not BLAME others for them.
6) If you are not willing to discard the victim card, you can't ever expect to play a winning hand! Drop the victim card and play the hand you are dealt!
7) Contrary to popular belief, our thoughts and feelings do not exist solely as random, spontaneous reactions to our surroundings; at least they do not have to!
8) Your dreams are your gifts from God. Following those dreams is your gift to God.

9) The time to pursue your dreams is NOW! When would NOW be a good time to start?
10) Everyone and everything in your life is there because *you* attracted them there. *You* placed the order with *your* thoughts. *You* paid the freight with *your* feelings and emotions. *You* signed for the package with *your* actions. *You* and only *you*! If you want a different result on the outside, you must first become a different you on the inside.
11) The "actions" to be taken in pursuit of one's dreams have more to do with "how" something is done than with the actual specific "whats" that are to be done.... In other words, it's the "hows" not the "whats" that matter most!
12) Again, it all boils down to creating and maintaining a certain **feeling** consistent with achieving your dreams.
13) In regards to thoughts, feelings and actions, your feelings reign supreme. They always, always, always win.
14) Boiling it all down to its inner, core essence, using the Law of Attraction to accomplish your dreams could be summed up in one six-word statement: **"Thoughts, feelings, actions supporting worthy goals."**
15) **"Thoughts, feelings, actions supporting worthy goals!"**
16) Often times, when we learn of a negative event, we are tempted to think to ourselves,

"Can you imagine that?" Don't do it! Don't let that toxic story become a part of you.

17) Maybe it's time to write a *new* story about yourself; one that actually supports your grandest dreams and aspirations. Change your story, change your thoughts, change your life!

18) Every time you re-live a past hurt, a past-perceived failure, you resuscitate it and give it life anew. If you want to create real, lasting change in your life, stop re-animating (re-living) past hurts and start re-scripting (visualizing) new successes.

19) You can sum up the Law of Attraction in one word: **FEELING!**

20) Thoughts may well become things as what you think about comes about, but *only* if you fuel it with feeling; deep, gut-level feeling.

21) The keystone to putting the Law of Attraction to work for you in the pursuit of your dreams revolves around replacing and/or up-leveling your underlying feelings about what you are thinking, saying and doing.

22) Remember, your thoughts, feelings and actions all play a role. But, your feelings set the overall tone. Think of your feelings as the train track that sets your course. Your thoughts and actions serve as the fuel cells for the train engine. Positive or negative feelings determine where the track is headed. Your thoughts and actions serve as the fuel cells made either of coal (if

they are in alignment with your feelings) or of water (if they are in opposition to your feelings). The one can power the train engine, really ramping up its power and speed. The other douses the fire and slows the engine to a crawl, sometimes even stopping it cold. But, only the direction of the tracks (your feelings) determines your ultimate destination.

23) Whatever situation you find yourself in, first seek to be specific about choosing the feelings you allow yourself to entertain.

24) Learning to "conduct" yourself now (remember the train analogy?) *how* you would if you already had your dream fulfilled is the key.

25) **In order for things to change and improve, you don't need a "change of venue." What you need is a "change within you!"**

26) Act "as if" what you are currently doing, whatever that is, actually matters. It does! Act "as if" what you are currently doing is taking you closer to your dreams. It is taking you somewhere either way! Act "as if" what you are currently doing is a necessary step in taking you toward your dreams. It is!

27) Learn to think, feel and act *how* you would if you had already realized all of your grandest dreams! Learn to BE the person who has already succeeded, before it manifests in the seen.

28) Get in the habit of only uttering that which supports your grandest dreams. If your dreams

were already realized, if you had everything your heart desires, *how* would you speak? Speak that way now!

29) **Make room in your life for your soul mate by making room for your soul mate in your life.**

30) **Make room in your life for your dreams by making room for your dreams in your life.**

31) Every one of us matters. It's up to each one of us, individually, to decide why.

32) Part of what makes goal-setting / goal-getting, striving and overcoming obstacles so powerful and so transformative is the leap of faith that it requires us to make. None of us knows for sure, upon embarking on any new journey, what the outcome will be. As such, it requires us to believe in ourselves, often well in advance of any concrete evidence in favor of such. In doing so, we catch glimmers of our own unlimited potential. Furthermore, the "distraction" of goal-setting / goal-getting, striving and overcoming obstacles gets us out of our own way. This process connects people, sometimes for the first time ever, with the *feeling* of their own intrinsic worth.

33) Conformity is the death knell to success.

34) Now, which do you think will move you closer to realizing your dreams: focusing on (and thus magnifying) your lack and perceived failures or

focusing on (and thus magnifying) your successes?

35) How will you even recognize your success when it presents itself if you never bothered to define it in the first place?

36) We are always attracting our ideal mates. It's just that the one(s) who are an ideal match for us at any given time are not always to our liking. Therefore, if you want to find/attract your "ideal" soul mate, you must first become the match to that which you seek.

37) The only way to attract a better relationship is to bring a better *you* to the table!

38) Consistency and congruency are the keys. Consider them "the C & C of success!" For example, seeking your "ideal" soul mate while simultaneously engaging in one-night stands is not congruent. The very act of going out, trolling for whomever you can find, sends a very different message than wanting to find your "ideal" soul mate.

39) Your dreams are not just for you! They are meant to be expressed and increased for the good of us all.

40) Find your afflatus!

41) Remember always: You Matter! Your dreams matter! And you are worthy *and* capable of following and achieving *all* of your dreams right NOW!

42) Been there, bled that!

43) Most people start their day with a daily dose of mindset poison by watching the news or reading the negative-themed stories in the newspaper. Be different from the rest to bring out your best!

iContractor1

Appendix E

Always Believe In Your Dreams Coaching (SM) Method Charts

In Chiropractic, there is a teaching tool from the 1920s referred to as the "Safety Pin Cycle." (1) Basically, the "Safety Pin Cycle" looks at the function of the nervous system and reduces it down into an easy-to-follow, closed-loop feedback mechanism that resembles a safety pin. At the top of the safety pin, you have a brain cell and at the bottom, you have a tissue cell. Nerves connect the brain cell and tissue cell together into a closed-loop feedback system. The motor nerves (efferent transmission) run from the brain cell to the tissue cell, telling the tissue cell what to do. Sensory nerves (afferent transmission) run from the tissue cell up to the brain cell, telling the brain cell about its environment. (see Figure I) For example, let's say that the tissue cell is in your hand. And, let's say that you put your hand onto a hot stove. The sensory nerves transmit information to the brain telling it that your hand is on fire. The brain responds by transmitting along motor nerves to cause muscles to contract pulling your hand from the hot stove.

This same analogy, the Safety Pin Cycle, can be used to explain the Always Believe In Your Dreams

Coaching (SM) methodology for applying the Law of Attraction. However, instead of having a brain cell at the top of the safety pin, let's put the "What" that you have decided you want. The bottom of the safety pin will now be your "How", your internal level of being. The motor nerves running from top-to-bottom, "What" to "How", reflect "How" you would feel if you already had succeeded in accomplishing your dream. We'll call this your "anticipated post-success feeling." The sensory nerves running from bottom-to-top, "How" to "What", we will call your "pre-emptive feeling." This is the "How" feeling, previously identified, that you now must create, in advance of your dream fulfillment. (see Figure II)

To really understand how the law of attraction operates, let's now turn the safety pin on its side. The bottom of the safety pin, the "How", now resides squarely in your heart, where all of your feelings originate. And the head of the safety pin, the "What", lies at the interface between your inner world (inner states) and outer world (outer events). This is where the frequency emitted by your thoughts, feelings and actions goes out into the Universe. And, let's place that "What" in the center of a bulls-eye to signify the laser-like focus, precision and clarity you are using by being exquisitely specific in describing exactly what you want. (see Figure III)

Finally, we plug the simple, 3-step Always Believe In Your Dreams Coaching (SM) methodology into our safety pin cycle, replacing the "anticipated post-success feeling" with "Up-level" and replacing "pre-emptive feeling" with "Act 'as if.'" (see Figure IV) Making sure your thoughts, feelings and actions are consistent and in congruence maximizes their attractive pull.

Now can you see why focusing your efforts on changing your outer world, rather than your inner world, is futile? As Mark Victor Hansen says, life "is an inside➔outing rather than an outside➔inning." (2) Changing your inner world first (and only) is what changes the quality and quantity of light you are emitting so that what gets *reflected* back to you is more in alignment with your innermost dreams and aspirations.

iContractor1

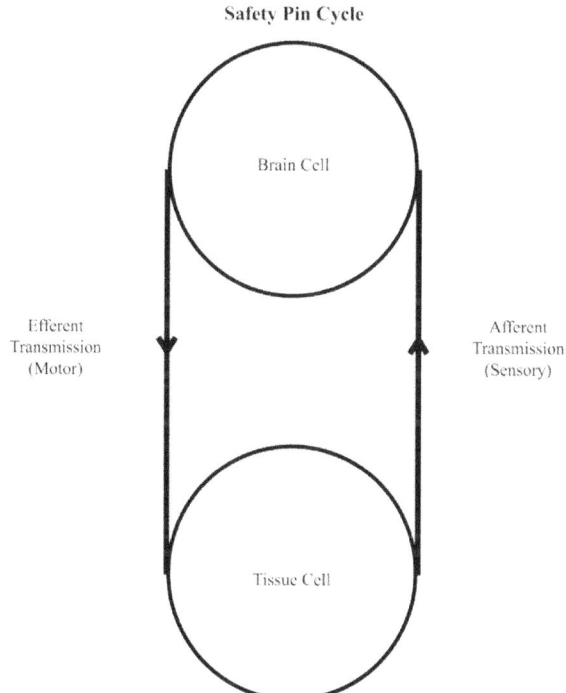

Figure 1

iContractor1

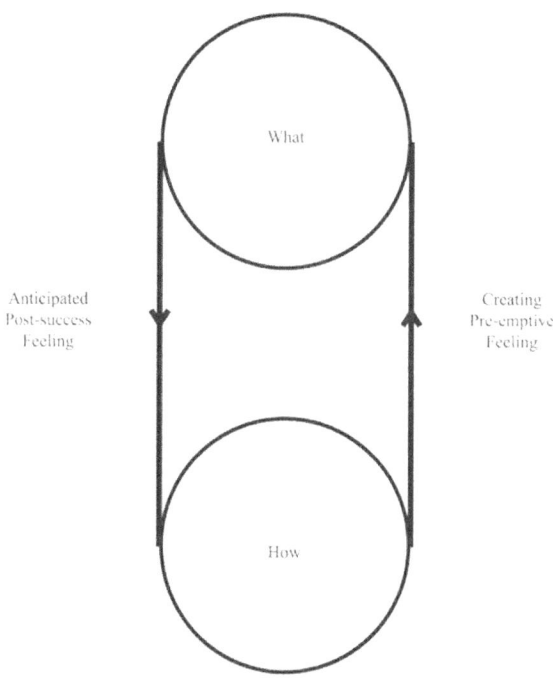

Figure II

iContractor1

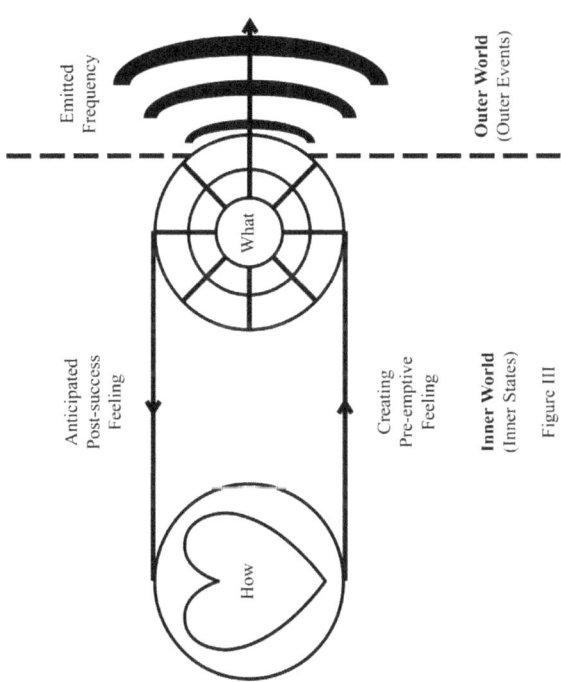

Figure III

iContractor1

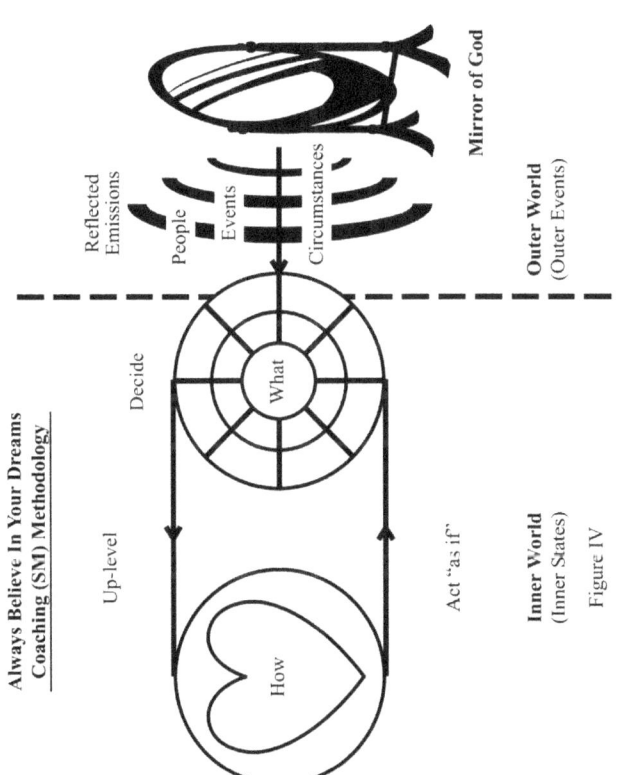

iContractor1

A Quick Note Concerning Quotes

As you can clearly see, I am a HUGE fan of quotes! In every instance, I have endeavored, to the best of my ability, to give credit where credit is due. This has not always been as easy as one might think. The following quote, for example: "How you do anything is how you do everything." This is one of my all-time favorite quotes. It shows up in T. Harv Eker's Secrets Of The Millionaire Mind on page 121. However, it also shows up in Jack Canfield's The Success Principles on page 100. Both books are copyright 2005. Because I first encountered it in T. Harv Eker's book, I gave him the credit.

The real value in quotes is not so much in who said what as much as it is in what was actually said. The beauty of quotes lies in their ability to reduce BIG concepts down into smaller, simpler, eloquent packets of wisdom that can trigger "Ah-ha!" moments of understanding. As Jim Rohn says, "Don't be afraid to borrow if someone else has said it well…You could stay up all night and not think of that." (1)

iContractor1

Sources

Opening Page

(1) Chitty Chitty Bang Bang (DVD)
(2) The Little Engine That Could, Watty Piper
(3) (3) Adapted from The Science Of Chiropractic, D.D. Palmer pp. 78-81

Introduction

(1) The Secret (DVD)
(2) Outliers, The Story Of Success, Malcolm Gladwell p. 40

"It's All Your Fault" - The Reason For The Season

(1) The Treasury Of Quotes by Jim Rohn, p.94

(2) Leading An Inspired Life, Jim Rohn p.95

Mirrors, Windows, Doors & Light

(1) Secrets Of The Millionaire Mind, T. Harv Eker p.15
(2) Success: Quotes For Achievers, Les Brown p.19
(3) The Law Of Success, Napoleon Hill p.271
(4) Man's Search For Meaning, Viktor Frankl p.66

iContractor1

(5) Count Your Blessings, Dr. John F. Demartini p. 212
(6) In Tune With The Infinite, Ralph Waldo Trine p. 33
(7) Bible, John 14:2
(8) Count Your Blessings, Dr. John F. Demartini p.29
(9) Neale Donald Walsch, daily e-mail newsletter 4/12/2011
(10) 10.) Think And Grow Rich, (Fawcett Crest edition, 1960), Napoleon Hill p. 55
(11) 11.) Feel the Fear and Do It Anyway ®, Susan Jeffers
(12) 12.) The Book Of Positive Quotes, John Cook p. 219
(13) 13.) Bible, Genesis 1:27
(14) 14.) Bible, John 8:12
(15) 15.) Bible, John 10:30
(16) 16.) This Date, From Henry David Thoreau's Journal, April 24, 1859
(17) 17.) Dr. John F. Demartini, Facebook posting 6/20/2011
(18) 18.) Step Into Your Greatness, Les Brown (DVD), track 1 of 7

The Law Of Attraction

(1) Think And Grow Rich, (Bob Proctor version), Napoleon Hill p. 226

(2) The Power, Rhonda Byrne p 35
(3) www.einstein-quotes.com
(4) Live Full And Die Empty, Les Brown (DVD)
(5) The Secret, Rhonda Byrne p. 73
(6) The Science Of Getting Rich, Wallace Wattles
(7) Secrets Of The Millionaire Mind, T. Harv Eker p. 121

Thoughts

(1) The Secret, Rhonda Byrne p. 9
(2) In Tune With The Infinite, Ralph Waldo Trine p. 18
(3) Conversations With God, Neale Donald Walsch
(4) The Answer Man (DVD)
(5) The Bigness Of The Fellow Within – Vol. XXII, B.J. Palmer
(6) The Land Before Time (DVD)
(7) Walden – Life In The Woods, Henry David Thoreau
(8) Reader's Digest, "Quotable Quotes", January 2004 p.63
(9) Illusions: The Adventures Of A Reluctant Messiah, Richard Bach p. 100
(10) The Law Of Success (1925 edition), Napoleon Hill p. 109
(11) The Strangest Secret, Earl Nightingale, (audio program, track 3 of 10)

iContractor1

Feelings

(1) The Power, Rhonda Byrne p. 81
(2) The Master Key System, Charles Haanel, Part Twelve, Number 18, p. 108
(3) Think And Grow Rich (Bob Proctor version), Napoleon Hill p. 335
(4) Think And Grow Rich (Bob Proctor version), Napoleon Hill pp. 68-69
(5) What Was I Scared Of?, Dr. Seuss
(6) Step Into Your Greatness, Les Brown (DVD), Track 3 of 7
(7) The Power, Rhonda Byrne p. 149
(8) The Answer, John Assaraf & Murray Smith p. 124

Actions

(1) The Science Of Getting Rich, Wallace Wattles
(2) In Tune With The Infinite, Ralph Waldo Trine
(3) The Science Of Getting Rich, Wallace Wattles
(4) Think And Grow Rich, Napoleon Hill
(5) The Secret, Rhonda Byrne
(6) The Treasury Of Quotes, Jim Rohn p. 3
(7) Think And Grow Rich, (Fawcett Crest edition, 1960), Napoleon Hill p. 55
(8) Dr. John F. Demartini, Facebook posting 8/7/2011
(9) Count Your Blessings, Dr. John F. Demartini p. 23

(10) Unlimited Riches, Mark Victor Hansen, (Audio Cassette Program, Tape 1A)
(11) Reader's Digest, November 1997 p. 89
(12) Fabulously Fit Forever – Expanded, Frank Zane pp. 139-148
(13) Bible, Luke 11:9-10
(14) Count Your Blessings, Dr. John F. Demartini p. 23

Supporting Worthy Goals

(1) The Strangest Secret, Earl Nightingale (audio program)
(2) Webster's New Universal Unabridged Dictionary, 1996 edition, p.2009
(3) Milo, Volume 18, Number 4, March 201 p.2
(4) "Secret Income System", Bob Proctor (on-line advertisement) and Bob Proctor's Insight Of The Day 01/31/2008
(5) The Meadville Tribune, cryptoquote, 4/23/2011
(6) Leading An Inspired Life, Jim Rohn p. 71
(7) Leading An Inspired Life, Jim Rohn p. 72
(8) www.thinkexist.com
(9) The Northern Light, August 2011, p. 27
(10) Neale Donald Walsch, daily e-mail newsletter, 4/21/2011
(11) Live Full And Die Empty, Les Brown (DVD)

Always Believe In Your Dreams Coaching (SM)

iContractor1

(1) <u>I'm Starvin'</u>, John Pinette (DVD)
(2) <u>The Power Of Focus</u>, Jack Canfield, Mark Victor Hansen, Les Hewitt p. 59
(3) <u>Blue's Clues</u>, Nick Jr. Productions
(4) <u>The Success Principles</u>, Jack Canfield p. 7
(5) Jack Canfield, Facebook posting, 2/12/2011
(6) <u>Secrets Of The Millionaire Mind</u>, T. Harv Eker p. 121

Afflatus

(1) Webster's New Universal Unabridged Dictionary, 1996 edition, p.34
(2) <u>Bible</u>, Matthew 25:14-30 and Luke 19:12-28
(3) <u>Bible</u>, Matthew 25:31-46
(4) The Meadville Tribune, cryptoquote 5/6/2011
(5) <u>The Strangest Secret</u>, Earl Nightingale (audio program)
(6) Per thinkexist.com, goodreads.com and answers.yahoo.com
(7) www.thinkexist.com
(8) John Assaraf Facebook posting 6/20/2011
(9) <u>Step Into Your Greatness</u>, Les Brown (DVD)
(10) <u>The Book Of Positive Quotations</u>, John Cook p. 275
(11) <u>Mr. Magorium's Wonder Emporium</u>, (DVD)

Afterward

(1) <u>Illusions: The Adventures Of A Reluctant Messiah</u>, Richard Bach p. 181

Appendix A

(1) <u>The Treasury Of Quotes</u>, Jim Rohn p. 8

Appendix E: Always Believe In Your Dreams Coaching (SM) Method Charts

(1) <u>Chiropractic Textbook, Vol. XIV</u>, R.W. Stephenson, p. 9
(2) <u>Unlimited Riches</u>, Mark Victor Hansen, (Audio Cassette Program, Tape 1A)

A Quick Note Concerning Quotes

(1) <u>The Treasury Of Quotes</u> by Jim Rohn, p.36

iContractor1

Bibliography

Assaraf, John, and Murray Smith. *The Answer.* New York: Atria Books (A Division of Simon & Schuster, Inc.), 2008.

Bach, Richard. *Illusions: The Adventures Of A Reluctant Messiah.* New York: Dell Publishing, 1977.

Live Full And Die Empty. Produced by Seminars On DVD (www.seminarsonDVD.com). Performed by Les Brown. 2006.

Step Into Your Greatness. Produced by Success Media (www.success.com). Performed by Les Brown. 2004.

Success: Quotes For Achievers. Dallas, Texas: SUCCESS Books by SUCCESS Magazine, 2008.

Byrne, Rhonda. *The Power.* New York: Atria Books (A Division of Simon & Schuster, Inc.), 2010.

The Secret. Produced by Prime Time Productions. Performed by Rhonda Byrne. 2006.

The Secret. New York: Atria Books (A Division of Simon & Schuster, Inc.), 2006.

Canfield, Jack. *Facebook Posting.* February 12, 2011.

The Success Principles. New York: Harper Collins Publishers, 2005.

Canfield, Jack, Mark Victor Hansen, and Les Hewitt. *The Power Of Focus.* Deerfield Beach, Florida: Health Communications, Inc., 2000.

Chitty Chitty Bang Bang. Produced by Metro Goldwyn Mayer. 1968.

Cook, John. *The Book Of Positive Quotations.* Minneapolis, Minnesota: Fairview Press, 1997.

Demartini, Dr. John F. *Count Your Blessings.* New York: Hay House, Inc., 1997; 2006.

Demartini, Dr. John F. *Facebook posting.* June 20, 2011.

Demartini, Dr. John F. *Facebook posting.* August 7, 2011.

Einstein, Albert. *Einstein Quotes.* www.einstein-quotes.com (accessed August 13, 2011).

Eker, T. Harv. *Secrets Of The Millionaire Mind.* New York: Harper Collins Publishers, Inc., 2005.

Frankl, Viktor. *Man's Search For Meaning.* Boston: Beacon Press, 1959; 2006.

Gladwell, Malcolm. *Outliers, The Story Of Success.* New York: Back Bay Books, 2008; 2011.

Haanel, Charles. *The Master Key System.* written in 1912 and published in 1916. Public Domain, 1916.

Hansen, Mark Victor. *Unlimited Riches.* 1995.

Hill, Napoleon. *The Law Of Success - Original 1925 Edition.* Beverly, Massachusetts: Orne Publishing, 2010.

Think And Grow Rich - The Original Version, Restored And Revised. Clemson, South Carolina: The Mindpower Press, 2004.

Think And Grow Rich. New York: Fawcett Crest Edition, 1960.

Mr. Magorium's Wonder Emporium. Produced by Twentieth Century Fox Home Entertainment. Performed by Dustin Hoffman. 2007.

Holmes, Oliver Wendell. *Think exist .com.* www.thinkexist.com (accessed August 2011).

Holy Bible.

Jeffers, Susan. *Feel the Fear...and Do It Anyway.* New York: Ballantine Books, 2006.

Johnson, Traci Paige, Todd Kessler, and Angela C. Santomero. *Blue's Clues.* Produced by Nick Jr. Productions. Performed by Steven Burns. 1996-2006.

Nightingale, Earl. *The Strangest Secret - How To Live The Life You Desire.* 1956.

Palmer, B.J. *The Bigness Of The Fellow Within - Vol. XXII.* Davenport, Iowa: The Palmer School Of Chiropractic, 1949.

Palmer, D.D., and B.J. Palmer. *The Science Of Chiropractic.* Fort Worth, Texas: Parker Chiropractic Resource Foundation, 1988.

"Personal Glimpses." *Reader's Digest Large Edition*, November 1997.

I'm Starvin! Produced by Levity Productions. Performed by John Pinette. Image Entertainment, Inc., 2006.

Piper, Watty. *The Little Engine That Could*. New York: Platt & Munk, Publishers, 1930.

Proctor, Bob. *Insight Of The Day.* January 31, 2008. www.insightoftheday.com (accessed January 31, 2008).

"Quotables." *The Northern Light*, August 2011.

Rohn, Jim. *Leading An Inspired Life.* Niles, Illinois: Nightingale-Conant Corp., 1997.

The Treasury Of Quotes. Southlake, Texas: Jim Rohn International, 1994; 2006.

Seuss, Dr. *Think exist .com.* www.thinkexist.com (accessed August 2011).

What Was I Scared Of? New York: Scholastic, 1961; 1997.

Stephenson, R.W. *Chiropractic Textbook - Volume XIV.* Davenport, IA: The Palmer School of Chiropractic, 1927.

Strossen, Randall J. "Trancendental Levitation." *MILO A Journal For Serious Strength Athletes* 18, no. 4 (March 2011).

The Answer Man. Produced by Magnolia Studio. 2009.

The Land Before Time. Produced by Universal Studios. 1988.

The Meadville Tribune. "Cryptoquote." April 23, 2011.

The Meadville Tribune. "Cryptoquote." May 6, 2011.

Thoreau, Henry David. *Walden - Life In The Woods.* 1854.

Thurman, Howard. *John Assaraf Facebook posting.* June 20, 2011.

Trine, Ralph Waldo. *In Tune With The Infinite.* Lexington, Kentucky: Seven Treasures Publications, 2009.

Unknown. "Quotable Quotes." *Reader's Digest*, January 2004: p. 63.

Walsch, Neale Donald. *Conversations With God.* New York: G.P. Putnamy & Sons, 1996.

Neale Donald Walsch. April 12, 2011. www.nealedonaldwalsch.com (accessed April 12, 2011).

iContractor1

Neale Donald Walsch. April 21, 2011. www.nealedonaldwalsch.com (accessed April 21, 2011).

Wattles, Wallace. *The Science Of Getting Rich.* Tuscon, Arizona: Iceni Books, 2001.

Webster's New Universal Unabridged Dictionary. New York: Random House Value Publishing, Inc., 1996.

Wilde, Oscar. *Think exist .com.* www.thinkexist.com (accessed August 2011).

Zane, Frank. *Fabulously Fit Forever - Expanded.* Palm Springs, California: Zananda, Inc., 1993.

Notes

iContractor1

Notes

Notes

iContractor1

Notes

Notes

iContractor1

Notes

Notes

iContractor1

Notes

Notes

www.ingramcontent.com/pod-product-compliance
Lightning Source LLC
Chambersburg PA
CBHW070607010526
44118CB00012B/1462